Kathy Peel & Joy Mahaffey

A Mother's Manual for SCHOOLDAY SURVIVAL

FOCUS ON THE FAMILY

PUBLISHING

Pomona, California

To our flexible, supportive and long-suffering husbands: Bill Peel and Mark Mahaffey, who will probably write a book entitled: How To Survive Living With Blooming Writers;

And to our children: John, Joel and James Peel, Kristi, Mac, Bill and John Mark Mahaffey, who thoroughly enjoyed eating fast-food meals while their mothers were writing.

A MOTHER'S MANUAL FOR SCHOOLDAY SURVIVAL

Copyright © 1990 by Kathy Peel and Joy Mahaffey

Library of Congress Cataloging-in-Publication Data

Peel, Kathy, 1951-
  A mother's manual for schoolday survival / Kathy Peel & Joy Mahaffy.
     p.   cm.
  ISBN 0-929608-88-7 : $7.99
  1. Creative activities and seat work—Handbooks, manuals, etc.   2. Family recreation—Handbooks, manuals, etc.   3. Amusements—Handbooks, manuals, etc.   4. Parenting—Handbooks, manuals, etc.
I. Mahaffey, Joy, 1949-   II. Title.
GV1203.P36   1990
790.1'91—dc20   90-36126
                                                                            CIP

Published by Focus on the Family Publishing, Pomona, CA 91799.
Distributed by Word Books, Dallas, Texas.

Adult supervision is suggested for the activities and recipes listed in this manual. Any employment of the creative ideas and recommendations made in the following pages is at the reader's discretion and sole risk.

Unless otherwise noted, Scripture quotations are taken from The Holy Bible, New International Version. Copyright © 1973, 1978, 1984 by the International Bible Society.

Edited by Sheila Cragg and Janet Kobobel
Designed by Sherry Nicolai Russell
Illustrations by Bruce Day
Printed in the United States of America

Copyrights and Acknowledgments (Listed in order of appearance in the contents.)
Introduction
Excerpt from *Speaker's Lifetime Library* by Leonard and Thelma Spinrad, © 1979, 194, used by permission of the publisher, Prentice-Hall, Inc., New Jersey.
Chapter 7
Excerpt from *Bits & Pieces* (January 1989), vol. 22, no. 1, 13, used by permission of the publisher, The Economics Press, Inc., 12 Daniel Rd., Fairfield, New Jersey 07006.
Chapter 10
Creativity (Dallas: Ann McGee Cooper & Assoc., Inc., 1988, 1989), 31.
Chapter 11
Burton Hillis, "The Man Next Door," *Better Homes and Gardens* (April 1990), vol. 68, no. 4, 166.
Chapter 12
"Age of Innocence," *Reader's Digest* (October 1989), 75.
Chapter 13
E.C. McKenzie, *14,000 Quips & Quotes for Writers & Speakers* (New York: Grenwich House, 1980), 501.
Chapter 15
Howard G. Hendrick's seminar on Creativity in Ministry.
Excerpt from *Bits & Pieces* (May 1989), vol. 22, no. 5, 8, used by permission of the publisher, The Economics Press, Inc., 12 Daniel Rd., Fairfield, New Jersey 07006.
Excerpts from *Webster's New World Book of Aphorisms* by Auriel Douglas and Michael Strumpf, © 1989, used by permission of the publisher, Arco Publishing, a Division of Simon & Schuster, New York.
Chapter 16
Leonard and Thelma Spinrad, *Speaker's Lifetime Library* (New Jersey: Prentice-Hall, Inc., 1979), 51.

90 91 92 93 94 95/ 10 9 8 7 6 5 4 3 2 1

Table of Contents

Acknowledgments

Our dream to write and to encourage parents has been realized because of the following people. They have shared their expertise and given us encouragement:

Sheila Cragg and Janet Kobobel, our patient and flexible editors, and the entire Focus Family, which has graciously and enthusiastically helped us at every turn.

Bill Peel, for getting us started on our survival projects.

Dan Johnson, for believing in our vision.

Judie Byrd, for allowing us to use many of her ideas from her School of Cooking and Entertaining.

We appreciate the following friends who have graciously helped and shared creative ideas with us:

Marilyn Ackerson, Liane Beacham, Suzanne Blair, Laurie Breedlove, Tim Brookshire, Susan Carroll, Thelma Ruth Childs, Alan Clay, Inez Colley, Ann McGee Cooper, Rene Cordell, Debbie Dalton, James Dobson, Kathleen Duff, Margaret Griffin, Jennifer Hall, Ron Hall, Karen Hampton, Gay Harvey, Karen Heaton, Howard Hendricks, Debbie Keuer, David Lawrence, Linda Lesniewski, Lisa Lesniewski, Laura Lightfoot, Dorothy McAuley, Ann Magoffin, Connie Newton, Laurie Pillsbury, Jeanne Rajabzadeh, Tom Ramey, Jr., George Ann Reed, Donna Ridenour, Josh Ritter, Jim Slaughter, Joan Smith, Terri Squyres, Carol Swaim, Gloria Tjoelker, Gene Thrash, Kathryn Waldrep, Dianne Williams, Amy Yahnig and Peggy Zadina.

We want to thank the following schools in Tyler, Texas, for providing creative examples and for testing our projects in their classrooms:

Caldwell Playschools, Hand in Hand Preschool, Andy Woods Elementary School, Grace Community School, Hubbard Middle School, Robert E. Lee High School, and Glenn Malone and the Rice Elementary School fifth-grade students.

Introduction

"In loco parentis—Latin for 'Children can drive their parents crazy.'"

We've often wondered why kids don't come with a warning label. Our prenatal classes didn't prepare us for Saturday morning with Rude Dog and the Dweebs, temper tantrums in the cereal aisle, broken hearts, hormones, peer pressure and seventy-five dollar tennis shoes. We do count our kids among our greatest blessings. We just wish someone had informed us that our bundles of joy would require an enormous amount of emotional energy.

Like most parents, we weren't equipped for computer programming, new math, old phonics or space-age science fair projects. We weren't warned that our cute little sports car would have to be traded in for a vehicle that resembles an orthopedic shoe, seats twelve and averages ten miles per gallon.

Rare is the mom and dad who enters parenthood with all the emotional and intellectual equipment needed to nurture their precious little bundles from the delivery room to the dorm room. Just look at the job description: Teach your kids good habits, responsibility, self-discipline and social graces. Help them with their education, physical skills and spiritual growth. Keep the kids clean and fed. Take them to thousands of ballet lessons, baseball tournaments, soccer games and school plays.

To help you survive, we have included in this manual hundreds of fun, easy-to-do activities for families with children in pre-school, public school and private school as well as those parents who home-school. We are convinced that with a little creativity, organization and sense of humor, many of the stresses, which cause our grip on sanity to slip, can be conquered.

As you strive to do your best at the age-old privilege and challenge of raising kids, we hope that this manual will give you some fresh ideas. We trust that it will help you create an atmosphere in your home that fosters creativity, learning, laughter and love.

Kathy Peel
Joy Mahaffey

Chapter 1

Preparing for the School Year

Our homes are just like yours—far from perfect. Like you, we regularly deal with kids crying, mates sighing and pets dying as we try to keep our homes sane and sanitary. We've used up precious emotional energy looking for that important paper John Mark was supposed to save but lost—and now his whole self-image rests on finding it.

Over the years, through both defeats and victories, we've learned that administrating a house full of people, pets and projects is a big job. If we want our seven kids—in pre-school, elementary school, middle school and high school—to start the school year on a positive note, we must plan ahead. Our get-ready-for-school lists alone run the gamut from crayons to compasses, lunch boxes to lipsticks.

Some of the following ways we prepare for the school year may help you:

**"Rulers, scissors, blunt of course,
Colored pencils, too;
Notebook paper, new lunch box,
Folders red and blue;
Gym shorts, backpack, tennis shoes,
I'm filling up my cart.
My checkbook tells me once again,
It's time for school to start!"**

1. Set up a family filing system to keep track of important school papers and future activities. Provide each person in the family with his or her own color file folder. For example, One child's could be blue, another one's orange, red or yellow. Keep your folders in a small, two-drawer filing cabinet. A cardboard box could also be decorated to hold the folders.

Label the folders for each child's activities or areas of need. At an early age, teach your children that the first thing they should do when they arrive home is to place important papers in their folders.

These are some of the folders high schoolers might need: sports team schedules, school notices or information, Scouting activities, church youth group events, coupons for favorite eating places or college or vocational school brochures. An elementary-age child might have folders for the school calendar, soccer team phone numbers, special papers or awards or church club activities. You may only need one colorfully decorated file for your preschooler. It's also fun to have a folder for pictures of things kids want to save money for, such as toys, sports equipment or video games; or for brochures of upcoming events, such as a concert, church or scout camp or other desired activities.

2. Place a large bulletin board in the kitchen and post appointment cards for the doctor or dentist, invitations, meeting notices, school schedules or sporting practice and game calendars. Teach your children to help you keep the bulletin board up to date. It also helps to record each person's schedule in a different color on a calendar with large blank squares. Otherwise, you may miss important birthday parties and sports events because they weren't entered on the calendar.

3. Hang a marker board in a heavy-traffic area. The kids can check it daily for assigned jobs, messages or reminders. Use the board for fun brain teasers, treasure hunt clues or words of praise.

4. Help your kids clean out closets and clutter. Pass on clothes and toys in good condition to other families.

5. Decide on a clothing and school supplies budget for each child. Then sit down with that child and make a list of needs, helping him or her consider the budget limit when making choices. If possible, take each child out individually to shop for school needs. Joy uses this time to talk over each child's fears and goals for the upcoming school year.

6. Before the school year begins, discuss expectations and schedules. Decide when homework should be done, how much TV will be allowed and what household work your children will be expected to do. If a young person's class load is going to be heavy, try to lighten their chores.

7. Go with your child to school a week before classes start to meet the teachers and to find out some of the subjects the class will be studying during the year. This is also a good opportunity to locate classrooms, obtain a list of school supplies and talk about where to meet the carpool or get on the bus. The Peels have a tradition of taking each teacher a loaf of homemade bread at this time.

8. If your child walks or rides a bike, go over the different routes to and from school. Locate homes of friends along the way where he or she could stop in case of an accident or emergency.

9. Sign up your children for a bicycle safety class. Watch your local paper to see who might be sponsoring a class in your city. (Many times, the police department does.)

10. If your children attend a school which has lockers, teach them how to open a combination lock before school starts. Then they will be able to open their locker quickly and not be tardy for class.

11. Teach your kids to make double use of their time. For example, do homework while waiting at the orthodontist's office or fold laundry while watching TV.

12. Create a system to motivate your kids to do their chores, extra reading, homework or to practice music or sports. Incentives help kids develop consistent work habits. (See Mom's Humdinger Reward Chart on page 6.)

13. Make a list of Saturday household chores, along with a set length of time in which they must be finished. When each child does his or her share, everyone has more time for creative activities. Try to make this time as much fun as possible. Many times the Peels rummage through the skit box for crazy clothing to wear, put on ugly wigs, play upbeat music and dance with mops and brooms while working.

(See our chapter with chore charts, "Getting a Little Help Around the House" in *A Mother's Manual for Summer Survival,* also published by Focus on the Family Publishing.)

Mom's Humdinger Reward Chart

Name _Joel_

Finish Line

Chores

Homework

Extra Reading

Music/Sports

Start

Grand Prize

Dinner for you and a friend at the pizza parlor.

Rules

Color one square per lane when you:

1. Complete your chores.

2. Finish all homework to the best of your ability.

3. Read ___30___ minutes in an approved book or magazine.

4. Practice ___piano___
(music or sports)

for ___30___ minutes.

Collect grand prize when you reach the finish line.

Mom's Humdinger Reward Chart

Name _____

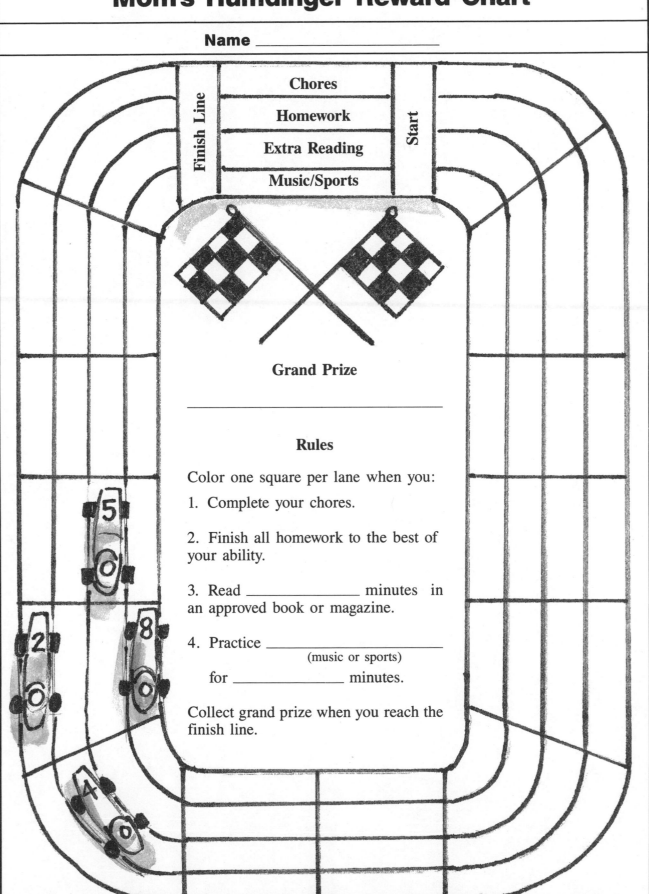

Finish Line

Chores

Homework

Extra Reading

Music/Sports

Start

Grand Prize

_____

Rules

Color one square per lane when you:

1. Complete your chores.

2. Finish all homework to the best of your ability.

3. Read _____ minutes in an approved book or magazine.

4. Practice _____
   (music or sports)

   for _____ minutes.

Collect grand prize when you reach the finish line.

Chapter 2

Rise and Shine

When you begin your morning by punching the snooze button five times, you've started the day with stress. Chances are everyone else in the family will start off grumpy, if they have to clear a path to the kitchen to hunt for something—anything—to eat.

The Peels prefer rising early, so their family can begin the day on a positive note. One morning a week Bill also takes care of the kids while Kathy shops for groceries at 5:45 a.m. She saves at least thirty minutes and a lot of headaches by shopping without the kids. The store isn't busy, and she avoids buying those extra candy bars and cookies that the kids try to hide under the sack of potatoes.

We're morning people, but you may be a night person. Just the thought of getting up one minute earlier may exhaust you. Kathy's sister, Marsha, has two preschoolers who are up at dawn. She would need to set the alarm for 3:30 a.m. to copy Kathy's schedule. Instead, Marsha accomplishes her household administration tasks the night before. It's amazing how much more she gets done when the kids are asleep.

Before the school year starts, discuss the tasks expected of each family member in the morning. (See the Rise and Shine Chart on page 11.) If chores are shared cheerfully, a lot more can be accomplished. Sibling bickering and parental nagging can be avoided by clearly defining tasks and setting time limits on when they should be completed.

Spending quiet time with God and reading inspirational material also makes a significant difference. Family unity is strengthened when you take out ten minutes to plan and pray together about the upcoming day. If work schedules make this difficult, this can be done at night.

The following ideas may also help your family rise and shine with a smile:

**"The sun is up,
my coffee's cold,
The kids and dog are fed.
I've done a full day's
work by nine,
I'm going back to bed!"**

1. Take the frozen juice out of the freezer and let it thaw in the refrigerator overnight; it will be easier to mix in the morning.

2. Set the table at night, and get out the necessary items you'll need for breakfast. For example, if you plan to fix waffles, put the waffle iron and the dry ingredients out on the counter.

3. Make sandwiches for lunch boxes the night before and store them in the refrigerator in self-locking sandwich bags; add the lettuce the next morning.

4. If the kids need to do chores in the morning, make a list they can follow and give it to them the night before. Younger children sometimes just need an easy system to know who is supposed to bring in the paper and who should feed the cat.

5. Make a rotating schedule for the bathroom; this will help eliminate some of the hassles. A vanity with a mirror in a teenage girl's room, where she can primp and put on makeup, can also spare bathroom bickering.

6. Purchase each school-age child an alarm clock with a pleasant tone or music. This helps children learn to take responsibility for their own schedules.

7. If possible, allow enough time in the morning for an unrushed breakfast. This is a great time to communicate as a family about the upcoming events that day.

8. Encourage your children to prepare for the morning the night before. They can decide what they'll wear and set it out. Designate an assigned place for school gear, so they don't have to play hide and seek at the last minute to find books or gym shorts.

9. Exercise in the morning; it helps get those creative and mental juices flowing.

10. Don't turn on the TV in the morning unless the older kids need to watch a special news report.

11. Make a sunshine jar for children who move slowly in the morning and tend to disrupt the schedule. Every day that they're dressed and ready for school on time, drop a quarter in the jar. They can use the money collected during the week for a Friday afternoon treat.

12. Whether you drive your children to school or send them out the door to ride their bikes or meet the bus, be sure your last words are positive ones. Joy parts with her children each morning by asking them for one particular prayer request she can remember during the day. Whether it is a history test at one o'clock or dealing with feelings of rejection from a friend, her kids know their mom is praying for them.

Rise and Shine Schedule

Week of _Sept. 10_

Children's Names	Kristi	Mac	Bill	John Mark	
Rise & Shine	5:45	7:00	6:30	7:00	
Bathroom Time	6:00	7:10	6:45	7:30	
Early Morning Chores	☑ make bed ☑ (Tues.) sort laundry ☑ make lunch	☑ make bed ☐ feed cat ☑ (Fri.) sort laundry	☑ make bed ☑ feed fish ☑ load dishwasher	☐ make bed ☑ help set table ☐	☐ _____ ☐ _____ ☐ _____

Rise and Shine Schedule

Week of _____

Children's Names					
Rise & Shine					
Bathroom Time					
Early Morning Chores	☐ _____ ☐ _____ ☐ _____	☐ _____ ☐ _____ ☐ _____	☐ _____ ☐ _____ ☐ _____	☐ _____ ☐ _____ ☐ _____	☐ _____ ☐ _____ ☐ _____

Chapter 3

Calling All Dads
by Bill Peel

Dads, there is no doubt about it. We have a responsibility to our children that can't be delegated to mothers. No gift, no opportunity, no other person, including mom, can substitute for a father's involvement with his children. Kids need our affection, affirmation, attention and example. They need us to drive them to ballet lessons, fix their bicycles, help with their school work, throw the ball to them, listen to their problems and be with them in their joys and pains.

"For unflagging interest and enjoyment, a household of children . . . certainly makes all other forms of success and achievement lose their importance by comparison."

Theodore Roosevelt

dividuality. Although Mark Mahaffey and I are fascinated by the uniqueness of our children, making adjustments for seven different personalities is sometimes taxing. What motivates one child doesn't work with the others.

Children need us to respect them for who they are, and they need us to set an example of warm, unconditional love; of consistent, appropriate discipline; of willing, compassionate forgiveness; and of a strong faith in and love

Ralph Mattson and Thom Black, in their book *Discovering Your Child's Design,* suggest that parents think of themselves as farmers. Our job is to cultivate a child's gifts and talents. Instead, we often act like architects, imposing our own design onto our children rather than letting them be themselves.

We fathers need to affirm our children's in-

for God that brings meaning to life. One of the common denominators found in healthy families is a spiritual commitment. Indeed, it is this focus on God that reminds us of the immense value of our remarkable children.

We dads can also be an example to our children in the upkeep and maintenance of the home. If we want them to learn that it takes everyone's help to accomplish household chores, they need to see us with a dishtowel in one hand and a toilet brush in the other. They need to see us take the initiative to change the next diaper, wash a dirty face, get up for the midnight feeding, make sack lunches or handle the next discipline problem without being asked.

Calling All Single or Divorced Dads

If you are a single dad or have remarried, you have a real challenge. While you are away from your children, you can stay in contact by writing short notes or letters regularly. Your messages of love and affirmation can be read again and again. Try to call at least once a week for an extended talk and update on their lives.

If you live near your children, get to know their teachers, coaches and friends. Attend your children's activities whenever possible, and be available to drive them to their various events. Some of the best conversations happen naturally while waiting at a red light.

All parents need help from time to time, but single parents find this need intensified. You might network with other single dads in your area. Get together regularly to share your victories and defeats, your successes and failures. Plan outings and day trips with other single dads and their children. Seek out relatives as support sources, especially older ones with child-rearing experience.

Help for All Dads

Though we have limited time to spend with our children, we can make the most of whatever we have. Look through the ideas section of this manual and jot down some fun activities to do with your kids after work. We have given more

to our jobs than we can afford to if we come home exhausted every night. Success bought at the price of neglected children is too high a price to pay.

The following guidelines and activities offer ways you can make your relationship with your children more meaningful:

1. Plan a night out for mom. Send her out to dinner with a friend or to shop while you cover the feeding, bathing and entertaining of the kids for the evening. Find out what your children want to do ahead of time and then do it together.

2. Make a time log and check how much time you are spending with each child. Chances are, if you don't schedule time for your children the same way you do business appointments, it will be easy for you to leave them out of your agenda. We have included a planning chart for you to reproduce and use. (See the Dad's and Kids' Calendar on page 18.)

3. Show interest in whatever your child is interested in, whether it's playing with clay or finding out more about the new blonde in algebra class. If at all possible, avoid giving your children busy signals when they are trying to talk to you. Otherwise, they will not only stop trying to communicate with you but will shut you out also.

4. Become involved in your child's extracurricular activities. Even if you must sit through a fairly mutilated "Minuet in G" by Beethoven, praise your child for trying. One dad told us that he had been involved in his girls' lives through field hockey, soccer, tennis, volleyball, and Indian Princesses, a father-daughter program at the

YMCA. You don't have to be proficient at all of these activities; just be interested because your kids are.

5. Let your child know you are proud of him or her. One dad framed his four-year-old's artwork and hung it on the wall of his office.

6. Help your children with their homework, rather than watching television while they're studying. If they don't need your assistance, let them know you are available. This will encourage those students to buckle down. One dad shared how he scheduled time in the evening just to help his kids with their homework. He was available to call out spelling words or help with math problems.

7. Admit you're wrong when you make mistakes or lose your temper. Kids don't need perfect fathers; they need ones who are honest and transparent. A father's genuine apology will knit him to his child's heart like nothing else.

8. Spend time with each child before he or she goes to bed. For my children, I created an imaginary friend, Angus McDonald, (pronounced McDoonald). Angus sings songs in a Scottish brogue and tells stories, then I pray with the boys.

9. Plan a special outing or trip alone with each child. Learn to identify the occasions that are important to him or her. Since women are usually more sensitive about this, ask for a little help. Take your wife to dinner and discuss the children's needs. One dad told us about planning a special day once a month with each of his children. Since

the father and his sons were interested in aquariums and ham radios, he often took them to the hobby shop. He took his daughter out for chips and a soda or a shopping trip. He stressed that this was not a time to discuss grades or needed behavior improvements, unless the child brought up the subject. He continued this monthly commitment until his children went to college.

10. Take your child out to lunch at least once a month or eat lunch with him or her in the school cafeteria. Mark goes to his kids' public school for lunch. I take our boys out for pizza. Check with your child's school regarding the rules for taking him or her off-campus for lunch.

11. Share a special occasion with your children at their school. For example, surprise your child with a birthday cake for his or her whole class. Let your child take you to school for Show-and-Tell, and talk about a hobby or your work. On the day that the Mahaffey's fourth child was born, Mark took a cake to his other children's classrooms so they could participate in the celebration. As a result, his son's kindergarten class drew pictures for the new brother. Another son's first-grade class made cards for the baby, and the daughter's fourth-grade class wrote letters about the important world events of the day.

12. Plan a trip with another father and daughter. One dad allowed his teenage daughter to plan a ski trip with a friend and her father.

13. Coach your child's baseball, soccer or other sports team. This is a great time to teach them the importance of being a good sport. That means

we need to model this behavior. You could also be a Scout troop leader or teach their Sunday school class.

14. Show that you care about your children's belongings. Designate a fix-it day. Let your kids choose one or two broken toys or a piece of equipment for you to repair together. If you are not the fix-it type, find a friend or neighbor you can trade skills with or take the cherished item to a repair shop.

15. Take an older child on a business trip. Mark has discovered it's an opportune time to visit without interruptions, and it's a learning experience for the child. Set some time at the end of the day for recreational fun.

16. Take your child to visit mom at work during her break, lunch or dinner hour. One dad regularly prepared a portable dinner and took his young daughter to see her mom at work in the hospital, where she was doing her gynecology and obstetrics residency.

17. Establish rituals your children will look forward to and will remember after they are grown. One dad cooks hamburgers every Saturday night, while another dad picks out the pumpkins in October and helps the kids carve funny faces. Another dad shines all of the shoes on Saturday night.

18. Measure your children's height regularly. Mark does this once a year on his children's birthdays. It's also fun to record their height at the beginning of the summer, when they often have a growth spurt, and then again before school starts to see how much they've grown. The back of a closet door is a good place to record their growth.

19. Take your children on overnight camping trips. One dad tells of the fun he has with his sons planning fishing and hunting trips. The trip is exciting but so is the anticipation while planning and packing. Kids feel a real sense of pride and accomplishment when they help provide the evening meal at the campsite. After the trip, have a family night to share and re-live the experience. A getaway with older elementary-age children is also a good time together to listen to Dr. James Dobson's tape series, "Preparing for Adolescence." (Available from your local Christian bookstore.)

20. Keep a do-it-yourself project going that you can work on with your kids. My boys and I have built a doghouse, bunk beds, a table for an electric train and a treehouse. We have also put up shelves in the kids' closets for their belongings, pursued wild inventions and worked on science fair projects. Quality time can be spent together dreaming about the project, drawing up a plan, taking trips to the store for needed materials, building the actual project, then enjoying the fruit of your labor.

21. Make albums and scrapbooks with your children, filling the books with memorabilia and photographs of your special projects, outings and trips together.

22. Teach your children to be well-rounded by exposing them to a variety of experiences. One

dad taught his son to appreciate fine antiques, then helped him furnish his room by haunting antique stores with him on weekends. This dad also wanted his daughters to know how to throw a baseball and catch a football, so he practiced these skills with them after school.

23. Help the kids take care of their pets. One dad spends time with his daughter this way. They have learned how to shear her Angora rabbit, give the dogs their baths on Saturdays and take their animals to the veterinarian when necessary.

24. Plan a simple celebration for a child's performance in a concert, school play or sports event. Surprise him or her with a congratulations card, flowers or a small gift. Stop on the way home for a frozen yogurt or a soda to acknowledge the child's effort.

25. Read aloud to your children. A teenage girl shared with us how she loved having her dad read Beatrix Potter books to her when she was small.

Dad's and Kids' Calendar

Week of _Oct. 6_

Monday	Tuesday	Wednesday	Thursday	Friday	Saturday	Sunday

Name _John_

Monday	Tuesday	Wednesday	Thursday	Friday	Saturday	Sunday
Out of	town	take to school	12:00 take out to lunch	Dinner together cook hamburgers	work in yard and clean garage / Fishing	church / family bike hike

Name _Joel_

Monday	Tuesday	Wednesday	Thursday	Friday	Saturday	Sunday
		take to school / attend football game		Dinner	work in yard and clean garage / Fishing	church / family bike hike

Name _James_

Monday	Tuesday	Wednesday	Thursday	Friday	Saturday	Sunday
		get materials for science project / 7:00 school program		take to school / Dinner	work in yard and clean garage / Fishing	church / family bike hike

Name _____

Monday	Tuesday	Wednesday	Thursday	Friday	Saturday	Sunday

Goals

1. Find something to praise each boy for daily.
2. Arrange Wednesday schedule to have more time for boys (since out of town Mon. & Tues.).
3. Do yard work and clean out garage early Saturday so we can go fishing.
4. Cook out hamburgers Friday night / rent family movie to watch together.

Dad's and Kids' Calendar

Week of _____

Monday	Tuesday	Wednesday	Thursday	Friday	Saturday	Sunday

Name _____

Name _____

Name _____

Name _____

Goals

_____

_____

_____

_____

_____

_____

_____

_____

_____

Chapter 4

Home Alone

The hours after school can be the most difficult part of the day—for the child and the working parent. The child is aware of the parent's absence, and the parent is concerned about how the child is doing.

You can make the best use of these after-school hours if you use the Home Alone Chart to plan the week. (See page 24.) You might want to reproduce it, mount it on cardboard and cover it with clear contact paper. Use an erasable marker pen, so you can use it again. Write in daily snacks, chores, homework you want your child to concentrate on, and special creative or play activities. Instruct your child to check off the appropriate space after he or she calls you.

To help make this a productive, good time for the child, consider the following ideas:

1. Allow your children to sit in on baby-sitter interviews and to have a say in the selection. They should like the person that is in charge.

2. Make a list of baby-sitter qualifications with your child. One mom and her son wanted a male caretaker, a college student who needed a part-time job and who enjoyed being with junior-high-age kids. The sitter needed to be an excellent role model and responsible. He should require that seat belts be worn in the car; he wouldn't leave her son home alone or have his girlfriend or other buddies over. He also needed to enjoy and participate in the activities the boy liked, such as golf and shooting baskets. The sitter needed to help with homework when necessary and see that chores were completed.

3. Set your own goals, expectations, house rules and safety precautions before interviewing a baby-

"When my mom went to work, she hired a college guy to take care of me after school. He shoots baskets with me and helps with homework. He's cool."

Jason, age 12

sitter. Make sure the person understands the importance of his or her role. The caretaker needs to know that you expect active participation in your plans for your children—not a sitter who sits in front of a TV all afternoon.

4. Let children help you make up a list of house rules. Be sure they know exactly what you expect of them. If your child is old enough to be unsupervised until a parent arrives home, be sure you have clearly communicated and written out the same information you would want a caretaker to know. Whenever possible, ask your child to call you when he or she arrives home. During the conversation, briefly discuss his or her school day, inquire about homework and go over afternoon plans. If you cannot be available for a phone call, make arrangements for your child to check in with a responsible person.

5. Plan some creative activities your children can do alone. Make sure you have all the supplies needed for the projects.

6. Decide what programs and how much TV will be permissible. Have the kids keep track of their TV time by maintaining a log.

7. If your kids are taken care of by a sitter, loan him or her your camera to take pictures of each child. That way you can capture precious moments you might miss while at work.

8. Surprise your home-alone child, by leaving special messages of encouragement or praise tacked to the bathroom mirror, TV screen, cereal box or school shoes.

9. Post a list of suggested snack foods on the refrigerator door. (See Chapter 8, "Scrumptious After-School Snacks.")

10. Collect no-bake recipes. Keep appliance use to a minimum, since burns are a major cause of household accidents.

11. Leave an easy-to-read list of emergency phone numbers and the names and numbers of friends and neighbors. (See the Home Alone chart on page 24.)

12. Don't put your child's name on the back of a shirt or on the outside of a backpack or school bag. A stranger could call out the child's name, making that child think the person is a friend of the child's parents.

13. Design a small emergency kit to keep in a backpack or purse. A small cassette tape box works well. Pack it with an extra house key, list of telephone numbers, quarters for the telephone and folded money for special transportation, such as a cab.

14. Have a family "code word" and a workable game plan for emergency situations. If you have asked an unfamiliar person to pick up your child from school, tell the person the code word so that your child will know it's safe to get in the car. This word should also mean "help" in case your child needs to call from a phone in a frightening situation. All he or she needs to tell you is the code word and location, and you'll get there as soon as possible.

15. Have a cabinet stocked with emergency medical supplies. Teach your child basic first aid skills. Many local hospitals offer courses for kids.

16. Discuss or role play these situations to help your child know what to do:

a. answering the phone and taking messages

b. going to a friend's house or having friends over

c. losing the house key

d. missing the bus or carpool

e. staying after school

f. choking, poisoning or accidental injury

g. fire, flood (burst pipes) or a natural disaster

h. someone hassles, threatens or makes sexual advances

i. stranger on the phone or at the door

j. weather emergencies

17. When you arrive home from work, ask specific questions about your children's day. Show that you are interested in their world. If you find it difficult to get more than an "uh-huh" or a "nope" for answers, use these questions to stimulate conversation:

a. What was your favorite class or subject today?

b. Tell me something interesting that happened to you today.

c. Who did you sit with at lunch?

d. Tell me about someone in one of your classes.

e. What are some of the upcoming events at school?

f. Do you have any new projects?

g. What can I help you with?

h. What happened today that you can be really thankful for?

Home Alone

Parent _Mom_ 566-3096
Neighbor _Smiths_ 581-8094
Neighbor _Johnsons_ 584-7042
Relative _Grandma_ 839-2071
Police _911_
Fire _555-3333_
Doctor _Dr. Rogers_ 531-3004

	Monday	Tuesday	Wednesday	Thursday	Friday
Call Parent (PHONE & ADDRESS BOOK)	✔	✔	✔	✔	✔
Snacks	mountain trail mix	popcorn in tin on cabinet	banana whip	cheese cookies	taco dip in fridge with chips or crackers
Chores	take out ☑trash unload ☑dishwasher sweep ☑kitchen floor	fold ☑clothes put ☑clothes away ☐	dust ☑furniture clean ☐room ☐	take out ☑trash ☐ ☐	water ☑plants unload ☐dishwasher ☐
Homework	work on science experiment	finish science poster	study for spelling test	4:30 band tryouts	
Play Activities	garbanzo bean architecture	5:30-6:30pm soccer practice	design airplanes from styrofoam	5:30-6:30pm soccer practice	McGee & Me videos

Home Alone

Parent _____
Neighbor _____
Neighbor _____
Relative _____
Police _____
Fire _____
Doctor _____

	Monday	Tuesday	Wednesday	Thursday	Friday
Call Parent	_____	_____	_____	_____	_____
Snacks	_____ _____ _____	_____ _____ _____	_____ _____ _____	_____ _____ _____	_____ _____ _____
Chores	☐ ___ ☐ ___ ☐ ___	☐ ___ ☐ ___ ☐ ___	☐ ___ ☐ ___ ☐ ___	☐ ___ ☐ ___ ☐ ___	☐ ___ ☐ ___ ☐ ___
Homework	_____ _____ _____	_____ _____ _____	_____ _____ _____	_____ _____ _____	_____ _____ _____
Play Activities	_____ _____	_____ _____	_____ _____	_____ _____	_____ _____

Chapter 5

Bored No More

Younger Children
Recipes

1. Lick 'Em, Stick 'Em Stamps and Stickers: Mix 2 teaspoons white liquid glue with 1 teaspoon white vinegar in a saucer. Use a small brush to paint the back of tiny pictures, pieces of artwork or old stamps. Lay the pictures out painted side up, making sure they don't touch each other. Let them dry completely, then lick and stick them. Children can design and color their own stickers for chore charts, school or decorations on gift bags. You can also use the stickers to make a collage. (This recipe is good for replacing the sticky on a stamp or envelope flap.)

2. Dinosaur Soap Bars: Stir 1 cup Ivory Snow and 1/3 cup water with a spoon to create a stiff dough. Mold mixture around a small plastic toy dinosaur, forming the soap into an egg shape. Allow the soap to dry until firm. It will take about seven days, depending on the humidity and the

"Homework's done; let's have some fun!"

size of the soap bar. (Use for hand washing only and not for bathing.)

3. Fruit Soup Party: In a blender, put one 10-ounce package of frozen raspberries, 3/4 cup orange juice, 1/2 cup half-and-half, and 1/3 cup sugar. Whip cream mixture on medium speed for a few seconds until smooth. Serve the soup in bowls. It is yummy! The kids can invite friends and their stuffed animals over for a dress-up party. Be sure to dress up the animals, too.

4. Penny Bath: Make pennies look like new by mixing 4 tablespoons vinegar and 1 teaspoon salt in a small bowl. Drop pennies into the solution. If the pennies don't instantly become clean, stir them for a minute with a wooden spoon, then polish them with a soft cloth and a drop of vegetable oil to make them shine. You can use shiny pennies as incentives for a good attitude or completing chores.

5. Doodle Paint: Mix 1/2 cup each salt, water and flour with 1 tablespoon cornstarch and 5 drops food coloring. Stir well. Pour into a squeeze bottle. Draw or paint on poster board by squeezing the bottle.

More Fun Things to Do

6. Let your child sort silverware, putting it in the correct compartments of the silverware tray while you're working in the kitchen.

7. Draw around cookie cutters on heavy paper. Color and cut out the figures. Use as bookmarks or for gift tags.

8. Play with magnetic letters or numbers on the refrigerator door.

9. Designate one low kitchen cabinet for plastic play dishes and empty cereal or oatmeal boxes.

10. Old socks are perfect for little hands to wipe off washable cabinet doors and tables. Provide a cleaning rag and a spray bottle with water for your helper.

11. Shave Like Daddy: Use an ice cream stick as a razor and nonmenthol shaving cream to shave along with Dad.

12. Pan for Gold: Bury pennies in a sand box. Your kids can search for the pennies, using plastic colanders or sieves.

13. Play Parachutes: Cut four eighteen-inch lengths of sturdy string. Tie one end of the string to each corner of a man's square handkerchief.

Thread the other end of all four strings through an empty thread spool and tie them to a paper clip. Wrap the strings and handkerchief around the spool. Toss it up in the air, and the parachute will unfold and billow out as it falls.

14. My Book Box: Help your child cover a medium-size cardboard box with colorful contact paper, or the child can draw pictures of his or her own and glue them to the box. This can be your child's Read To Me Box. Use it to store favorite books and ones checked out from the library.

15. Coupon Hunt: Give your preschooler the coupon, which matches the product you plan to buy in a specific grocery store aisle. Ask him or her to match the picture on the coupon to the product on the shelf. Cereal, canned goods, detergents and paper products are usually the easiest to find.

16. Raindrop Art: Fill empty salt shakers or spice bottles with dry tempera paint. Sprinkle a little of the powdered paint on cardboard or poster board in a modern art design. Use a spray bottle to squirt water on the picture. Let the paint dry, then shake off the excess powder. (Cover the work area with newspapers before doing this project.)

17. Sandbox Drawing: Make an inside sandbox. Use a large metal baking pan or sturdy shallow box. Line the bottom of the box or pan with foil and about two inches of cornmeal, salt or sand. This is a good way to help young children learn to draw alphabet letters, numerals and their name. A child can also practice spelling words. Draw-

ing pictures in the sand is fun, too. This activity is especially helpful for children who write their letters backwards or have difficulty reading or writing.

18. Balloons on a Blustery Day: Tie long strings to the neck of blown-up balloons. Kids love to run outside with them.

19. Jump the River: Draw two lines about a foot apart for toddlers and two feet apart for pre-schoolers. Pretend there is a river between the lines. See who can jump the river without getting his or her feet wet.

20. Tricycle Traffic: Construct road signs out of poster board and attach them to sticks or dowel rods. Plant the signs in cans filled with dirt so they will stand up straight. Design a highway on the sidewalk or patio with masking tape. Position road signs along the marked roadways. One child can pretend to be the policeman and direct traffic, while the other children ride tricycles or wheel toys.

21. Cloud Watching: Lie on a blanket in the backyard with your child. Look at the clouds and see if you can pick out the shapes of animals, faces or objects.

22. Sewing: Secure a piece of burlap in a large embroidery hoop. A young child can use a large darning needle with yarn to learn to sew. Begin by showing your child how to pull the needle and thread in and out of the cloth. Then teach your child how to follow a simple line design drawn on the burlap.

23. Animal Safari: Hide your preschooler's stuffed animals around the house—under the bed, peeking around a chest, inside a cabinet or in a closet. Turn off all the lights and use a flashlight to go on a safari to capture the animals.

24. Leaf Walk: Go for a walk with your young child, and collect leaves of varying colors, shapes and textures. Identify the different colors, examine the veins and talk about the different shapes of the leaves.

25. Stained Glass Leaf Pictures: Let your child place leaves between two pieces of waxed paper. Then spread a sheet of plain white shelf paper (not self-stick) under and on top of the waxed paper and press it with a hot iron until the waxed paper sticks together. (The shelf paper protects the iron.) When cool, tape the leaf picture to a window.

26. Leaf Creatures: Glue leaves to a large piece of drawing paper. Look at the shapes of the leaves, and then draw around them to create animals, adding arms, ears, legs, noses, trunks or wings.

27. Raking Leaves: Preschoolers enjoy raking leaves and stuffing them into bags. Let the kids jump into piles of leaves and throw them in the air. You'll have to do more raking, but the fun will be worth it.

28. Paper Chains: Cut colored construction paper into one-inch-by-five-inch strips. Show your child how to glue one end of the strip to the other to form a ring. Put another strip through the ring and glue the ends together. Repeat this

process to make a paper chain. These chains make nice table or party decorations. Hang balloons on a chain. It is also fun to string a chain from the top of the door frame across a child's room to the opposite wall.

29. Glue different shapes of dry macaroni to the lid of a small cardboard box. Spray paint the box a favorite color.

30. Check at a school supply store or ask a teacher for a model of the alphabet in correct print form. Your child can copy it to practice printing.

31. Your child can record his or her own stories on a cassette tape. Send the tape to grandparents. Ask grandparents to send a cassette back with stories of their childhood.

32. Buy sample carpet squares at a flooring store for a nominal price. Children enjoy jumping from one square to another. Put a carpet square under the dining room or kitchen table for a special place to sit and read books or have a snack. Play circus animal trainer; line up stuffed animals on carpet squares.

33. Balloon Catch: Blow up a balloon as big as the diameter of your kitchen funnel. Toss the balloon in the air and try to catch it in the wide mouth of the funnel.

34. Matching Numbers: Cut the numbered squares from an old calendar. Have your child match the numbered pieces to the numbers on a whole calendar page, line the numbered squares in the correct sequence, or use them to play

addition or subtraction.

35. Tearing Paper: Tear up junk mail and old magazines into shapes or strips. Glue the torn pieces of paper to colored construction paper for a collage. Because tearing paper helps preschoolers develop finger dexterity, the outcome of this activity is not as important as the process.

36. Matching Designs: Using ice cream sticks, make a design such as a rectangle, square, triangle, or tree without leaves. Then let your child copy the same design with his or her sticks.

37. Handprints: Help your young child make a plaster of paris handprint. Put 1 cup water in a disposable bowl. Slowly add 2 cups plaster of paris, gently allowing it to sift through your fingers. Wait about 5 minutes; then stir with a spoon until thickened like soup. Pour plaster into a disposable aluminum pie pan or a heavy paper dinner plate. Wait until the plaster is almost set but still tacky to the touch. This will take about 15 to 20 minutes, depending on the humidity and temperature. Then press the child's hand with fingers spread open in the plaster to make an impression. You may want to add the year, the child's age and first name below the handprint. Wash hands, and let imprint dry completely for 24 hours. Remove the plaster from the pie pan or plate; then your child can paint the handprint with acrylic paints. Attach a self-sticking picture hanger on the back of the plaque. Younger children may enjoy doing a footprint, too.

38. Follow the above directions for plaster of paris, pouring it into a disposable pie pan or heavy

paper plate. Make a picture with nature items. When the plaster is almost set, press a leaf vein-side down to make an imprint, then remove it. Push acorns, rocks or seeds into the plaster. Let it dry, remove plaque from the pan and attach a hanger to the back of it.

39. Paperweight: Following the plaster of paris directions, fill a small disposable pie pan to the brim. Push sea shells into the plaster when it is still tacky. Remove the pie pan after it is dry.

40. Make quick costumes from old pillowcases. Help your child cut a hole for the neck and arms. Use markers, acrylic paints, scrap fringe or lace to decorate the pillowcase. Ribbon or heavy yarn can be used for a belt. Pretend characters are unlimited.

41. Have an indoor picnic on a cold or rainy day. Spread an old quilt on the floor. Your children can imagine you're in an exotic place; describe what you might be doing or seeing if you were there.

Younger and Older Children

42. Soap and Sawdust Sculpture Clay: Stir 1/2 cup Ivory Snow into 1/2 cup water until mixture is thick and creamy. Then whip it with a spoon until the soap is stiff and fluffy. Gently fold in 2 cups of sawdust. Mold into animal or people figurines; airplane, car or boat models; or modern art sculptures.

43. Painted Desert Jars: Pour 1/2 cup salt into a pie pan. Rub a piece of chalk sideways against the salt until it is completely colored. Gently spoon colored salt into a small baby food jar. Repeat this process with different colors of chalk, adding new layers of salt to the jar until it is full. Fasten lid tightly. Use jars for paper weights. Larger jars make nice bookends. (Be careful; if the jars are shaken too much, the layers of colored salt will mix together.)

44. Write down the stories that your children make up for fun, or encourage them to write their own. Keep a spiral notebook in a convenient location. One mother from Puerto Rico told us that after Hurricane Hugo devastated their island, she bought her four girls notebooks and pens. They wrote stories and drew pictures during the cleanup. These notebooks have become priceless treasures.

45. Snow Jar: With a hole puncher, have your child cut as many holes as possible out of a piece of waxed paper. Or use 1 tablespoon of glitter instead of the waxed paper circles. Put the glitter or small circles of paper into an empty baby food jar. Use waterproof glue to cement plastic animals, figures or miniature flowers to the inside of the lid. Fill the jar with water. On the inside rim of the lid, apply a layer of glue and fasten the lid tightly. Allow it to dry, and then shake the jar.

46. Tin Can Stilts: Use two, forty-six-ounce, empty juice cans with both lids still intact. On opposite sides of the can close to one end, punch two holes with a pointed can opener. Thread six feet of clothesline rope through the holes and tie

them together with a knot. Do the same on the second can. Grip the knotted end of each rope, stand on the cans, and pull the rope up as you step. The smaller the child, the smaller the can and the shorter the rope. This is a great balancing exercise for children. (This activity is recommended for children five years or older.)

47. Treasure Hunt: Post clues, such as pictures, words or silly rhymes to direct your kids from one location to another until they find the treasure. Use picture clues for preschoolers, and let them hunt for their afternoon snack. Your kids will enjoy hunting for a birthday gift, money for an ice-cream cone, coupons for miniature golf or other special treats.

48. Kick the Can: Use an empty soup or vegetable can for this old favorite, making sure the edges of the can are not sharp. Set the can on a special spot on the sidewalk or driveway. Choose a child to be "it." The child who has been chosen closes his or her eyes and counts to fifty while the other children hide. The child who was chosen yells, "Ready or not, here I come." Then he or she goes out and looks for the other children. When one of the hidden children is spotted, the child who was chosen hollers, "One, two, three, I see Bill (name of child seen)." The child who has been seen and the chosen child try to outrun each other to the can. If the one who was hiding kicks the can first, he or she is safe. If the chosen child kicks the can first, the other child is considered captured, and the can is put back on the base. When one of the hidden children feels it is safe to run to the base and kick the can, he or she can try to do this. If the chosen child

sees someone running in and beats them back to the can, then that person is captured. After all the children are spotted, the game begins again. The child who was captured first is now the one to be "it."

49. Paper Dolls: Cut out full-length pictures of models from catalogs. Glue the models onto poster board and cut around the shape of the paper doll. For a doll stand, use a small ball of clay flattened on the bottom or make a slit in a styrofoam block. Stand the doll in the clay or styrofoam. Cut out clothes for the doll from the catalog, making sure to cut tabs on the shoulders and side seams to fold over and attach to the doll. Some children might enjoy designing and drawing clothes for their dolls.

50. Flannel Board Stories: Cover a piece of cardboard about two-by-three-feet with plain white or light blue flannel for a storyboard. Your child can cut out animals, people or objects from catalogs or magazines and glue flannel on the back of them. You can also use white interfacing, available at fabric stores, and trace animals, characters or objects from favorite storybooks or from coloring books. Color the interfacing characters with crayons. Make up flannel board figures for favorite stories, and keep the figures and stories in a large envelope. Storytelling is an excellent way to help children develop language skills.

51. An old but usable typewriter is fun for younger and elementary-age school children. They will enjoy picking out letters, spelling their names and words they know. Show older children

how to place their fingers on the keys. If you can find a simple typing textbook, let them try some of the exercises so they can learn to type properly. Elementary-age children may enjoy making up stories, writing notes to friends or letters to grandparents.

52. Save Christmas cards. Your children can cut out the pictures and greetings to create cards of their own. Older children can write their own Christmas poems and thoughts; look at the greetings on commercial cards for examples. Fold a piece of colored construction paper in half; glue pictures on the front and the greeting on the inside. Add glitter, ribbon and stickers for that extra touch. You can also make gift tags out of old cards.

53. Walnut Turtle Races: Scrape the meat out of walnut halves. Put a marble underneath each walnut half. Hold the walnuts and marbles at the top of a small ramp or table that can be gently tilted (a card table works well). Count, "One, two, three, go!" Release the turtles and watch them race each other down to the finish line at the bottom of the table or ramp. Decorate the turtles with colored markers, or glue feathers or glitter on the outer shell. The sillier they look the better. (Warn children not to put marbles in their mouths.)[1]

54. Photo Collage: Help your children select small school pictures or snapshots you have taken of them over the years. They can apply paste or glue to the back of the photos and stick them to heavy poster board or a sheet of cardboard. Frame the collage and hang it, or give it to grandma as a gift.

55. Golf Ball Art: Ask Dad for his old golf balls. Put a thin layer of tempera or acrylic paint in a disposable pie tin and roll a ball around until it is covered. Place a piece of plain paper at the bottom of a box. Pick up the paint-covered golf ball with a large spoon, and put it into the box. Lift up the box, and roll the ball around. Dip another ball into a different-colored paint and roll it over the paper. (Protect clothing with a large apron or one of dad's old dress shirts.)

Fun Things to Do With an Empty Oatmeal Box

56. Discard the box top, punch two holes in opposite sides of container, one inch from top. Cut an eight- to ten-inch piece of heavy yarn or twine to make a handle. Carry treasures in the box, such as tiny toys, acorns, leaves or rocks.

57. Punch holes in the lid. Put a thin layer of dirt, grass and twigs in the bottom of the box to make a home for insects.

58. Use acrylic paints to color a piece of construction paper with your school's name and colors. Glue the decorated paper around the oatmeal box. Store art supplies in the box.

59. A parent cuts the oatmeal box container into two-inch circles with a serrated knife. Your child can use the circles for fences or circus rings when playing with small plastic animals.

60. Use the two-inch rings to make a bottle toss game. Try to toss the rings over twelve-ounce soft-drink bottles filled with water and tightly capped.

61. Paint the outside of the oatmeal container

with festive holiday or seasonal colors. Make your favorite batch of homemade cookies, wrap them in clear plastic or colored cellophane paper, and put them in the box. This makes a nice gift for a friend, neighbor or teacher.

62. Make a bank. Cut a slit in the lid. Glue construction paper and scrap fringe around the box to decorate it.

Things to Do With Clothespins

63. Clothespin Architecture: Use clip clothespins, attaching one to the other to build houses or skyscrapers. (Clip clothespin activities are only recommended for older preschoolers.)

64. Write the alphabet or numbers on clothespins with a black marker. Clip pins together in sequential order or use for arithmetic problems. Make more clips with extra vowels and popular letters for spelling words. Clip the pins around the edges of a shoe box to store them. This is an excellent activity to help children develop finger dexterity.

65. Refrigerator Magnets: Draw a small picture of a butterfly, flower or object. Color the picture, cut it out, and glue it to one handle of a clip clothespin. Attach a magnet to the back of the pin with glue. Put the clothespin magnet on the refrigerator to hold artwork, cartoons, messages or photographs.

66. Ornaments: Glue small Christmas stickers or pictures from old cards onto clothespins, and clip them onto the Christmas tree.

67. Make an Advent calendar, using twenty-five clothespins. Cut out the numbered squares of an old calendar page, and glue each number to the pincher end of a clothespin. You can also glue a Christmas sticker on the pin as a decoration. Cut a piece of cardboard into the shape of a pine tree. Color the tree with markers or cover it with wrapping paper. Punch a hole in the top of the tree, thread a five-inch piece of string or yarn through the hole, and tie it for a hanger. Clip the clothespins around the outer edges of the tree. Attach a special treat to the clip, such as a small piece of candy, gum or a dime. Beginning December the first, remove a clothespin every day until Christmas.

68. Place Cards: Use cellophane tape to attach a piece of wrapped candy to one handle of a clothespin. Make nameplates from index cards. Clip each card to a clothespin, and set them at dinner plates for holidays, parties or just for fun.

69. Make cookie and chip bag clips. Write "Chips" or "Cookies" on the clothespins with colored permanent markers. A set of these clips makes a nice gift.

70. Set an empty coffee can on the floor. Stand with toes touching the can, hold clothespins at chest level and see how many you can drop into the can. Go for ten out of ten. It is also fun to stand back from the coffee can, and see how many pins you can toss into it.

71. Set up an art gallery. Cut a piece of clothesline to stretch across one wall of a child's bedroom. Tie knotted loops at each end of the

line, then mount cup hooks at both ends of the wall, so that the pictures are at the child's eye level. Attach the clothesline loops to the hooks, and hang great works of art with clothespins.

72. Make miniature dolls with wooden clothespins. Attach pipe cleaners for the arms; use cloth scraps for clothing. Draw faces with a pen or marker, and glue on strings of yarn for hair. To have the doll stand up, mount it in a small ball of clay. Clothespin figures can be used in centerpieces, school projects or for 3-D dioramas (scenes with sculptured figures, buildings or nature setting displayed in miniature).

73. Make a planter: Paint about twenty wooden clothespins with acrylic paint. Punch small holes in a clean tuna can on opposite sides near the top. String sturdy picture wire about twelve inches long through the holes to form a handle. Slip the painted clothespins all the way around the edges of the can. Fill the can with household plant soil, which will hold the pins in place. Plant a small ivy in the soil.

Fun Things to Do With an Old Sheet

74. Paint a mural on an old sheet, using acrylic paints. Children might enjoy drawing and painting animals, dinosaurs, a nature scene, school logo or sports event.

75. Put up a tension rod between a wide door frame; hang and pin a sheet over it as a stage curtain. Lower the rod and sheet for a puppet theater.

"Kids love new high-tech toys, They beg for the latest gadget, But for hours of creative play, An old sheet works like magic."

76. Make a flag: Cut the sheet into the desired shape. Decorate it with markers or acrylic paints. Staple the flag to the side of a fort or hang it from a treehouse.

77. Make shadow pictures by thumbtacking a plain white sheet to the top of a door frame. Turn a bright light on behind the sheet. The performers stand between the light and the sheet and act out a pantomime, an impromptu play, or use their hands to form alligators, ducks or rabbits for the audience.

78. Create costumes with a sheet. Add a rope belt, and act out Bible stories.

79. Make a tablecloth out of a sheet. Have friends sign their names, draw pictures with markers or make handprints on the cloth. (Protect your table; put newspaper under the sheet beforehand.)

80. Spread a sheet out on the floor before playing with building blocks or other small toys. When it is time to clean up, gather together the edges of the sheet, lifting it so all the pieces fall together in the middle, and dump the toys into a box.

Fun Things to Pretend

81. Clothing Store: Collect play clothes, old hats, jewelry, shoes, scarves, ties, large paper or plastic grocery sacks and play money. Arrange the merchandise on pretend counters, then buy and sell the items.

82. School: Set up a special place as a schoolroom, using the following items: chalk, chalkboard, crayons, erasers, colored and regular pencils, pens, rulers, storybooks and workbooks with age-appropriate exercises. Take turns playing teacher and students. Or your child can pretend to be the teacher, and stuffed animals can be the students. School activities can include drawing pictures and displaying them, grading papers or writing numbers and letters on the board. Use stickers for awards on art and work papers.

83. Office: Children can pretend to answer a toy telephone, type on an old typewriter and take notes on a pad of paper. Provide pencils, paper, old letters, junk mail and envelopes. Use a shoe box with a slit cut in the top as a mailbox.

84. Airplane: Set up chairs in two rows, leaving a center aisle. The two front chairs are for the pilot and copilot. Use old belts for seat belts. Provide plastic dishes, suitcases and trays. Someone can pretend to be a flight attendant and serve snacks. Others can dress up like people on a business trip or like parents traveling with children.

85. Library: Set up temporary shelves, using cardboard boxes turned sideways to hold the books. Use old rubber stamps, index cards for due-date cards, pencils and paper. Pretend to stamp books. Remind your children not to mark in the books. Take turns pretending to be the librarian.

86. Hospital: Make doctor's or nurse's uniforms out of old white dress shirts. White towels or cardboard will make a nurse's cap. Inexpensive bandages, cotton balls and water will help make washable dolls feel better. Old sheets can be torn into bandage strips to wrap around a doll's or a stuffed animal's broken arm or leg.

87. Service Station: Make a gas pump from a medium-size cardboard box. Cut a hole on one side large enough to insert a four-foot piece of old water hose. Push a long nail through the end of the hose inside the box, making sure the nail sticks out on both sides of the hose, so it won't slip out of the hole. Make a second hole to hold the nozzle. Paint the box to resemble a gas pump, and bring out the cars and trucks for a fill-up.

88. Rainy Day Walk: Play music and dress up in raincoats. Get out your umbrella, walk around the house, and imagine what you could see if you were outside. Jump a puddle, climb a hill, kick the water, feel the raindrops, listen to the thunder or discover animals hiding under a bush. Then get out some paper and paint a rainbow after

your imaginary walk.

89. Restaurant: Make a menu and a restaurant sign. Use aprons, chef's cap, plastic dishes and silverware, play money and toy cash register. Put an artificial flower in a vase on a card table covered with a tablecloth. Pretend to be a cashier, cook, waiter or waitress. Serve dolls or stuffed animals a snack.

Ideas for Older Children
Recipes

90. Rice Potpourri: Add 10 drops of food coloring and 10 drops of scented oil to 1 cup of uncooked long-grain rice (not instant). Put scented rice in a jar, tighten the lid and shake well. Pour rice into a pretty bowl, and enjoy the fragrance in your room. You may want to add a few drops of oil every two weeks.

91. Homemade Salt Beads: Mix 1 cup salt and 1/2 cup cornstarch in a medium saucepan. Gradually add 1/2 cup boiling water, stirring constantly. Add 1 drop food coloring and 1 drop perfume oil. Put saucepan on the stove and continue stirring mixture over low or medium heat for about 2 minutes. Allow the salt dough to cool for 3 to 5 minutes. Take a teaspoon of the dough and roll it into a small bead. If the mixture begins to crumble and dry out, moisten hands slightly when forming a bead. Stick a straight pin through the center of the bead, pushing the bead up near the head of the pin. Stand the pointed end of the pin in a styrofoam block or meat tray turned upside down. Allow the beads to dry overnight. Carefully remove the pins from the beads. String beads into bracelets or necklaces, using nylon fishing line or heavy-weight thread. Make sure the string is long enough to fit over a child's head or arm before tying the knot. Cut off any excess line. (Don't make the necklace too long because it tangles.)

92. Mapping Salt: Mix 1 cup salt with 1 cup regular white flour in a medium bowl. Add 2/3 cup water, and stir until the mixture is as thick as icing. Add 3 drops or more of food coloring, depending on the shade of color desired. You can also paint the dough with poster paint after it has dried. On a board, shape moist dough into hills, valleys, oceans or rivers to make a topographical map or a 3-D diorama. Drying time will be determined by the thickness of the map or diorama.

93. Taffy: Combine 2 1/2 cups sugar, 1/2 cup water, 1/4 cup vinegar, 1 tablespoon butter or margarine and a dash of salt in a large saucepan. Cook mixture over low heat, stirring gently until sugar dissolves. Cover pan and cook over medium heat 2 to 3 minutes. Remove cover, stir occasionally, and continue cooking over medium heat until the syrup comes to a boil. Use a candy thermometer to check the temperature. When the syrup reaches the hard ball stage (250 degrees), remove it from the heat. Pour candy onto a buttered jelly roll pan. Dribble 1 teaspoon mint or vanilla flavoring over the candy, and gently stir it in with a fork. Allow candy to cool to the touch. Butter hands, and pull taffy until light in color and difficult to pull. Divide candy in half, pull it into a rope, cut it into 1-inch pieces and wrap them in waxed paper. This recipe makes about 40 pieces of taffy.

Other Fun Things to Do

94. Garbanzo Bean Architecture: Soak garbanzo beans (also called chick peas) overnight. When beans are soft, drain the water. Insert a round toothpick or a wooden skewer into the rounded side of a bean. (The bean can split, so be careful when inserting the toothpick.) Attach another bean to the other end of the toothpick. Continue adding toothpicks and beans to form structures. Make objects for fun or for school projects. You can make castles, domes, squares, Ferris wheels or abstract structures. Great fun for all ages.

95. Designer Book Covers: Use plain shelf paper or paper bags for book covers. Cut paper to fit the book cover. Dip small brush or sponge into acrylic paint. Quickly dab the sponge on the bag, or flick the brush over the paper to splatter paint. (Cover work area with newspaper, wear paint clothes, and do this activity outside.)

96. Splatter acrylic paint on an old pair of white tennis shoes. Draw designs on shoelaces with paint pens.

97. Personalized Backpack: Paint pictures and designs on the packs with acrylic paint pens. Your children will enjoy using their packs to carry books to school, clothes to a friend's house for an overnight visit or supplies for a church, club or Scout meeting.

98. Skit Box: Collect crazy hats, funny wigs, ugly ties and zany clothes for plays, skits or just for fun around the house. Secondhand and thrift stores are great places to find costume items.

You'll be surprised how many times they'll come in handy for oral book reports, student government campaigns or youth group skits.

99. Bigger and Better: Divide into two or more teams of two to eight players. Give each team a penny. Set a time limit of forty-five minutes, then send the kids into the neighborhood to ask neighbors if they'll give them an item in exchange for the penny. The kids then take the item they received to a second house, and ask if they'll give them something bigger and better in trade. The team that comes home with the biggest and best item wins. Don't be surprised if they return with some big white elephants.

100. Grapevine Wreaths: Your child can decorate a small grapevine wreath to hang on his or her bedroom door. Change the decorations with the seasons. Use floral wire to attach the following items to the wreath: silk flowers for spring, hearts for Valentine's Day, dried flowers and plastic fruit for Thanksgiving or holly and pine cones for Christmas. You can usually purchase these items at hobby or craft stores.

101. Hanging Planets: Make planets to hang from the ceiling of a bedroom. Blow up one balloon for each planet and tie a string to each one. Cut newspaper into one-inch-by-eight-inch strips, then dip each strip into a bowl of liquid starch. Place wet newspaper strips on balloon until entire surface of balloon is covered. Let dry. Repeat this process, adding one or two more layers of newspaper; make sure the entire surface of the balloon is covered. Stick a pin through paper to pop balloon. The round shape remains.

Paint to represent each planet and hang from the ceiling with a thumbtack. Help your child look at the solar system and discuss the differences between the planets.

102. Baby-sitting Kit: Make up a box filled with creative projects for little ones. Include some of the easy crafts from this book. (Young people can take this kit with them when they baby-sit.)

103. Fictionary: Choose one person to start off the game. The chosen player looks in the dictionary for an obscure word that he or she thinks no one else will know. The player writes down the definition of the word, makes up three more believable definitions and then reads them aloud. The other players vote on which definition they think is correct. The ones who vote for the correct definition earn one point; each person keeps his or her own score. If the chosen player bluffs everyone, he or she earns five points. After everyone in a large group has had his or her turn, add up the points. The one with the highest score wins. If you only have two to six players, designate a winning score to aim for, such as twenty points. (Junior high and high school kids enjoy playing this game at home or with their youth group.)

104. Treasure Boxes: Make a birthday or get-well gift for a friend. Use acrylic paints or paint pens to monogram the top of a plastic box that has small compartments. These boxes can be purchased at a craft, hobby or fishing department of a store. A young girl's box could include candies, jacks and a ball, jump rope, play jewelry or makeup. In a boy's box, you might put balloons, baseball cards, a small bouncy ball, crayons, gum balls or marbles.

105. Sugar Cube Buildings: For school projects, build castles, fences, forts, historical buildings, monuments or pyramids out of sugar cubes. The cubes are used as bricks, graham crackers as the roof or shutters, small candies or licorice sticks as trim. Twigs can be used as trees and artificial grass as the ground. White coconut makes snow. Use white liquid glue to cement the sugar cubes and other trim together. This is fun to create, but it isn't edible.

106. Scratch designs on waxed paper with a toothpick. Write a message, and give it to a friend to hold up to the light and read it. Be careful not to tear the waxed paper by writing too hard.

107. Lay a sheet of waxed paper over colored comic strips and rub surface with the edge of a coin or a spoon. An imprint of the comic strip will appear on the waxed paper.

108. Personal Lap Board: Have a parent cut a piece of plywood twelve-by-sixteen inches. Sand the edges of the board. Your child can choose favorite photos or school pictures of friends. Paint the board and glue a few pictures on one side of it, or cover the entire board with pictures. Then laminate the top and back of the board with clear contact paper.

109. Make your own bulletin board. Cut a two-by-three-foot piece of heavy cardboard from one side of a box. Cut a piece of fabric, which is about three inches longer and wider than the board.

Fold the fabric over the edges, and secure it to the back of the board with masking tape. Punch two holes in the top of the board about twelve inches apart; use colored yarn or heavy cord to make a hanger. Use thumbtacks or stick pins to tack awards, pictures, phone numbers or schedules to the board.

110. Airplanes: Buy an inexpensive balsa wood airplane model. Use the pieces as a pattern, and draw around them on a large styrofoam meat tray. Cut the styrofoam pieces out, and assemble the airplane, following the directions for the balsa wood plane. When the airplane crashes, save the good pieces and make more planes. You can also design your own planes out of styrofoam trays.

111. Learn to braid: Fasten scraps of cloth, yarn or old nylon hose to a doorknob, and teach your child how to braid. Girls enjoy braiding their doll's or their friend's hair.

112. Trivets: Use a small brush and acrylic paint to draw designs on an inexpensive, ceramic-tile square. When dry, spray the tile with acrylic top coat, then glue felt to the back.

113. Stained Glass: Add four drops food coloring to two tablespoons water in the cup of a muffin tin. Make different colors in each cup. (Cover your work area with newspaper to protect it.) Dampen a coffee filter with water. Use an eye dropper to draw up the colored water, then squirt it on the filter. Wait until each color is completely absorbed before adding more. Allow the filters to dry. Tape the stained glass filters on a window. You can also make flowers out of the colored filters. Gather one filter together in the center and wrap the end of a pipe cleaner around it to make a stem. Line a plastic strawberry basket with a piece of colored tissue paper and set a styrofoam block inside it. Push the pipe cleaner stems into the foam and arrange the flowers.

114. Draw five ovals and turn them into objects, such as faces, fishes or flowers. Next draw five rectangles, squares or squiggly lines and make more pictures. This is a good imagination stretcher, and it is a fun way to keep a child entertained while waiting in a doctor's office.

115. Juice Can Earrings: Paint colorful designs with acrylic paints on six-ounce juice-can lids. (Don't use lids that require a can opener because the edges are too sharp.) Purchase earring clips or studs at a craft store and glue one on the back, in the center-upper-half of each lid. A hot glue gun works best.

116. Covered Button Earrings: Purchase snap-on buttons that are made to be covered. Remove the center wire. Cover the button with a fabric that matches a favorite outfit. Snap on the back of the button, and glue an earring clip or stud to it. These buttons can be purchased at craft or fabric stores.

117. Design your own maze: Draw a simple shape, such as a ball, car or dinosaur, or use a simple illustration in a coloring book. Now draw a maze inside the outline, including a system of roads, detours and blocked entrances. Be sure to mark the start and finish points. Give the maze to a friend and see if he or she can figure out the route.

118. Home Movie Theater: Rent a good movie, make your own invitations, and hand them out to friends. Serve popcorn in plastic cups and a favorite beverage. You can also check your local public library for free movies and a projector to rent. This is a great activity for bad-weather days.

119. Write and illustrate your own book of good jokes and tongue twisters. Share it with a friend.

120. Tin Pan Art: Draw a design on a piece of paper that fits inside a disposable, aluminum pie pan. Tape the design to the inside of the pan. Set it on a cutting board. With a hammer and nail, gently pound holes, outlining the design on the paper. Space the holes about one-quarter to a half-inch apart. When the design is complete, remove the paper. Lace or ribbon glued to the outside rim of the pan, and a yarn loop taped to the back as a hanger will give it the finishing touches.

121. Help your child learn fractions by having him or her slice cake, pie or pizza, or cut up apples, carrots or oranges in halves, fourths, eighths or sixteenths. Create math word problems to solve, using the number of people you are feeding and the amount of food you are serving.

122. Check available volunteer services in your community, such as a hospital or library, where your teens can serve.

123. Throw Pillows: Turn an old team jersey or T-shirt into a pillow. Sew up the neck and sleeve openings. Stuff the shirt with old panty hose or polyester stuffing available at fabric stores. Then sew up the bottom opening of the shirt.

124. Slumber Party Pillow Cases: Provide each child with a plain pillow case as a party favor. The children can autograph each others' pillow cases, draw crazy designs or pictures or write silly sayings with fabric paints.

125. Become a weather watcher, and chart the changes. Read the temperature at the same time every day for two or three months. Check the newspaper to see how your temperature reading compared. Chart the temperature on a graph, watching for patterns.

126. Design your own game board for Monopoly. Use the original game as a pattern. Make new property cards, and draw the layout of the game board on poster board, substituting your own hometown and neighborhood businesses for the properties. Play the game according to the original rules.

127. Backyard Golf: Make a three-hole golf course in your backyard. Place thirteen-ounce coffee cans on the ground sideways, and lay the cans out like a golf course. Use a plastic baseball bat and a whiffle ball or tennis ball. Start about ten feet from the first can; count the number of swings it takes to hit the ball into each can. The child with the least number of swings wins.

128. Nature Mobile: Find a stick or twig between twelve and fifteen inches long. Cut sturdy string into six- to twelve-inch lengths. Tie acorns,

dried leaves, small pine cones and seed pods to one end of the strings. Tie the other ends to the branch, and make a hanger for the mobile.

129. Batting Practice: Drill a hole through the center of a baseball. Thread a long piece of rope through the hole in the ball and knot it. Tie the other end of the rope to a tree limb so that the ball hangs down to about waist height of the child. Now the child can practice swinging a bat and hitting the ball, and it will always come back.

130. Tennis Ball Puppets: Cut a slit across an old tennis ball. Outline the slit with a red marker for a mouth. Draw a nose and eyes and glue yarn on for hair. Squeeze the back of the ball to make the puppet talk.

131. Top Spinning: Learn how to spin a top. Time how long the top spins, and try to break your own record. Hold a family or neighborhood top spinning contest.

132. Checker Shoot: Use masking tape to make starting and finish lines about ten feet apart on a tile floor. Place a checker on the start line. Snap the checker with your finger and see how close you can get to the finish line. The checker that comes the closest but doesn't go across the line wins.

133. Write for free information about the national parks in America. It's a fun way to learn about different parts of the country. The address is: Department of the Interior, 1849 C Street, NW, Washington, D.C. 20240.

Insects and Crawly Creatures

134. Cocoon or Caterpillar Box: Look for a caterpillar or cocoon attached to shrubs or tree branches. Break off a small branch, and put it in a plastic storage box along with the cocoon or caterpillar. Cover the box with a fine mesh screen folded over at the sides. Add fresh leaves for the caterpillar every day from the same type of tree or bush you found it on. Take out a book on caterpillars from the library to study. Check the box daily, and when the butterfly or moth emerges from the cocoon, release it.

135. Worm Jar: Use a shovel to look for earthworms under leaves, heavy mulch or damp soil. (Be careful to watch for snakes.) Fill two-thirds of a quart jar with mulch, loose dirt or potting soil. Mix in one teaspoon of cornmeal, add the earthworms, and cover them with dry leaves or a bit of newspaper to keep moisture in the soil. Punch small air holes in the jar lid and close the jar. Tape a black piece of construction paper around the jar, except when observing the worms. It is fun to watch them tunnel through the dirt. Keep the jar in a cool dry spot. Add 1/4 cup water and 1/2 teaspoon cornmeal twice a month. Change dirt every six weeks, and count the babies. Identify the eggs, which look like small, round, yellow seeds.

136. Cricket House: Find crickets in the yard or purchase them at a bait shop. Make a home for the crickets in a plastic storage box (the size of a shoe box). Use mesh screen for a lid. Place a small, water-soaked sponge in a jar lid. Put a branch and some cracker crumbs in another lid. Lay a small empty soup can on its side to give

the crickets a dark place to hide. Crickets hibernate in the winter, so they are available during the spring, summer or fall. Keep the crickets outside, since you don't want them to escape in the house. Tell the temperature by observing the crickets and using this formula: Count the number of cricket chirps per minute. Write down the number and subtract forty from it. Divide this number by four, then add fifty. Compare this sum with the temperature on your outdoor thermometer. Be prepared for some good laughs, trying to count cricket chirps.

Fun Family Ideas

137. Celebrate the first day of the month; make a special dessert. The Mahaffeys often bake a giant chocolate chip cookie on a pizza pan. Decorate the cookie with icing, and write the name of the month on it.

138. Learn geography and history at the dinner table. Parents and older children make up questions about a subject a younger child is studying. Try to stump each other. It is also fun to see who can most quickly name the capital of a state.

139. Global Search: The first person names a city, state, nation, mountain, ocean or river on a globe and hands it to the next person. That person must find and point out the location on the globe. After the place is found, he or she chooses a different location and passes the globe to the next person to guess. Continue the game until everyone has had a turn or two. This is a good way to learn geography and use a globe.

140. Stock Market: Teach older children about the stock market and how stocks are bought and sold. One family member is appointed the broker. He or she distributes $10,000 of play money to each player. Check the financial page of the newspaper, and have each player decide which stocks to buy. Once a week, evaluate the stock market together, recording the ups and downs of the stocks. Determine whether to buy more stocks or to sell existing stocks. Evaluate the positives and negatives of long- or short-term investments. Play for two months, and then see whose investment earned the most.[2]

141. Feathered Friend Watching: Build a bird feeder together as a family. Hang the feeder outside a window where it can be seen easily. Keep on hand a field guide on birds, looking for the ones that frequent your feeder. Record what birds come and the time of day.

142. Family Band: Each person imitates the sound of an instrument using only his or her mouth, hands or feet. Pick a simple tune, and play it on your instruments.

143. Reading Charades: Write the title of books on slips of paper, choosing ones your children know. Fold the papers, and put them in a bowl. One person draws a slip of paper and pantomimes the title. Whoever guesses the correct one has the next turn.

144. Help your child splatter paint a wall in his or her bedroom. Be sure to wear paint clothes and protect floors and furniture with plastic tarps. Paint one wall with a solid color of latex paint. Select two or three complementary colors. Then

use a medium-size brush to flick paint on the wall one color at a time. Allow each color to dry before applying another one.

145. Play word games such as Boggle, Probe, Scrabble and Spill & Spell, which will help children build spelling and vocabulary skills.

146. Once a month, when the weather permits, plan to get away with your family for a cookout at a nearby lake or park. Discuss school and workday experiences, share concerns and fears and talk about how to solve problems that have arisen in the family. And encourage each other.

147. Select a worthy nonprofit organization to help as a family. The project could be as simple as saving aluminum cans, selling them and donating the profits. It could also be as difficult as spending a Saturday weeding and mowing lawns or painting the organization's building.

148. Start special collections that your children will cherish when they grow up. Collect coins, Christmas ornaments, ceramic figurines, favorite books, historical memorabilia, sports cards or any things your children especially enjoy.

149. Adopt a single person, an older couple who don't have children nearby or a single-parent family. Include them in special family events or holidays. Help them with house repairs, errands, food, toys or clothing for the children.

150. Learn a few sign language phrases as a family.

151. Indoor Racquetball: You'll need two wire clothes hangers, old panty hose, masking tape and two narrow strips of cloth about twelve inches long. Pull the clothes hanger into the oval shape of a racquet, and bend the wire hook into a handle. Cut off one leg of the panty hose, and pull it over the wire racquet and handle until it is taut. Gather the hose up over the end of the handle, tie a knot in it, and cut off the excess hose. Wrap a cloth strip tightly around the handle, then bind it completely with masking tape. Make another racquet, blow up balloons, find a partner, and have some great fun.

152. Party Helpers: When mom and dad are having an adult party, the older kids dress up and help with the party. Use fabric paint to make white T-shirts look like tuxedos. They can also draw mustaches on their faces or wear fake ones. Old top hats are fun, too, or they could wear costumes that match the theme of the party. This is when the skit box comes in handy. The kids could serve food, play doorman and help ladies from their cars.

1. Marguerite Kelly, *The Mother's Almanac II: Your Child from Six to Twelve* (New York: Doubleday & Co., Inc., 1989), 332.
2. Ibid., 151.

Chapter 6

Don't Sweat the Small Stuff

See if you can relate to any of these "Murphy's Laws for Parents":

1. The tennis shoes you must replace today will go on sale next week.

2. Leakproof thermoses—will.

3. The chances of a piece of bread falling with the grape jelly side down is directly proportional to the cost of the carpet.

**"As you travel through life,
Whatever your goal;
Keep your eye on
the doughnut
And not on the hole."**

Anonymous

7. The item your child lost, and must have for school within the next ten seconds, will be found in the last place you look.

8. Sick children recover miraculously when the pediatrician enters the treatment room.

9. Refrigerated items, used daily, will gravitate toward the back of the refrigerator.

4. The garbage truck will be two doors past your house when the argument over whose day it is to take out the trash ends.

5. The shirt your child must wear today will be the only one that needs to be washed or mended.

6. Gym clothes left at school in lockers mildew at a faster rate than other clothing.

10. Your chances of being seen by someone you know dramatically increase if you drive your child to school in your robe and curlers.

Here are some ways your family can laugh together and develop a positive atmosphere in your home:

1. Cut out funny cartoons or comic strips and share them with each other. Post them on a

bulletin board or the refrigerator door.

2. At the dinner table, read a chapter from Martha Bolton's book about family life, *"If Mr. Clean Calls, Tell Him I'm Not In!"*

3. Cut others—as well as yourself—some slack. Don't expect perfection. Laugh at mistakes, then get up and go on.

4. If you're experiencing stressful times as a family, do some physical activities. Go biking, swimming, walking or do aerobic exercises. Exercising helps work out the tension, gives you more energy and makes you feel better.

5. Do something nice for someone who needs encouragement. When we do kind gestures for others who are hurting, it helps us realize that we aren't the only ones with problems.

6. Try our frown remover recipe: Look at someone else or look in the mirror and frown. That takes seventy-two muscles. Now try smiling; it only requires fourteen muscles.

7. Draw funny faces on the bottom of each other's feet with washable markers. Be ready for lots of tickling and laughter.

8. Laughter is contagious. Start with one family member saying, "Ha." The next one says, "Ha, ha," continuing around the table, each person adding a "ha," until you lose track of who's on what "ha."

9. Create and record your own repertoire of funny songs and crazy rhymes. Loosen up and enjoy yourselves. Your silly ditties will become family treasures. One of the Peel's sons still loves to hear—in private, of course—the nonsense songs his parents sang to him as a baby.

10. Choose a game your family enjoys playing. Decide how long you'll hold the contest (for example, two weeks or a month). Keep a running score. At the end of the allotted time, the losers serve the winners to a special treat that has been decided in advance. One year the Peel family conducted the Blonds vs. Brunettes Tournament. The Brunettes conceded when the Blonds far outscored them. They took pictures and put together a special tournament album.

11. Fill your mind with positive thoughts from good literature, especially the Bible. Our subconscious is like soil that accepts any seed, good or bad, and then proceeds to grow what has been planted. Psychologists confirm what God's Word has said for more than 2,000 years: "For as he thinks within himself, so he is" (Proverbs 23:7, NASB).

Chapter 7

120 Miles and Still in Town

Many afternoons we actually clock 120 miles driving kids to various activities—all on opposite ends of town, of course. Some days our hands feel permanently glued to the steering wheel. We feel we've more than earned our chauffeur's badge by carpooling cranky, hungry kids who growl at anything that moves and bounce all over the car like tennis balls.

One afternoon, Kathy heard a lot of commotion from the back seat that sounded stranger than usual. When she pulled over to settle the problem, she discovered that the baby's "gross drooling," as the kids called it, had caused another child to throw up. Kathy rushed them to her pediatrician's office, thinking she had a car full of sick kids. The doctor told her, "The kids are fine. You need a car wash worse than a doctor!"

The following ideas have helped us turn those miserable miles in the car into a somewhat enjoyable adventure:

"A well-adjusted parent is one who can enjoy the scenery even with the kids in the back seat ."

Anonymous

1. Before you pick up the kids, try to take a fifteen-minute refresh-and-relax break. Read a chapter from a book or a magazine article. While you're driving, listen to inspiring or soothing music.

2. If you do errands while carpooling, plan ahead to save time and frustration. Make a list of the places you need to go, and map out a route to avoid backtracking. Call to see if a specific product is available or ready for pickup. It's no fun rushing into the pharmacy only to find out they didn't fill your prescription because they were missing simple information.

3. Prevent squabbling in the car by planning ahead. Change the seating arrangement monthly, so the kids won't argue over who sits where. And keep kids who don't get along separated from each other.

4. Provide activities or games and some nutritious snacks to tide kids over after school, especially if you're going to be in the car an extra-long time. They won't be nearly as crabby.

5. Bring along a bag of candies, cookies or gum to reward courteous, cooperative behavior.

6. Keep a pair of sunglasses in the car for each one of the children. In the afternoon, the bright sunshine causes headaches and sets off short emotional fuses.

7. Carry small dolls, cars, crayons or books in a lunch box for your preschoolers. Let them pick out the toys they want to take along. Add a surprise to their box once in a while.

8. Play street sign bingo. Cut out six-by-eight-inch cards from poster board. Draw and color your own signs or cut out pictures and glue them on the cards. School supply stores, motor vehicle license handbooks and some police stations have booklets with pictures of signs. Cover bingo cards with clear contact paper. When you play the game, use washable markers to check off the signs.

9. Make up a math game from speed limit signs. If the speed limit is thirty-five, then ask your child to add three plus five or for multiplication three times five.

10. Set up a rotation system, so each child may choose the music or story tape to be played during the drive. While listening to music, try to identify the instruments. Our kids enjoy classic fairy tales, Mother Goose rhymes and the *Adventures in Odyssey* tapes produced by Focus on the Family. We've also found that they become so involved in the story they don't bug each other as much.

11. Ask your preschooler to tell you when the traffic signal changes from red to green.

12. Teach art education on the go. Look for four kinds of lines: circle, curve, dot or straight. Highway stripes are straight; rooftops have angles; roads are curved; traffic signals are dots; open manholes are circles. Preschoolers can learn to identify shapes by looking at road signs.

13. If your child has had a hard day, stop for a soda pop or an ice cream and talk it over. Or stop for an unexpected treat to say, "Thank you for being such good kids!"

Chapter 8

Scrumptious After-School Snacks

Whipping up a delicious treat is a great way to spend time with your kids after school. Use these moments to talk about the day's events, as well as to teach some basic cooking skills.

Some of these recipes require parental help and careful supervision:

Super Snacks

1. Kids' Nachos: Cover a baking sheet with foil. Put a layer of tortilla chips on the sheet, sprinkle with grated cheddar cheese, and broil about one minute until cheese is melted.

2. Sprinkle a bowl of popcorn with Parmesan cheese. One mom pops corn every afternoon, and her kids enjoy the appetizing aroma as they come in the door.

3. Fill celery stalks with cream cheese, peanut butter or pimento cheese.

4. Stir 1/4 cup Grape Nuts cereal into an

"Your child's after-school hunger quotient is inversely proportionate to the number of snacks you have on hand."

8-ounce carton of flavored yogurt for a crunchy treat.

5. Put a slice of cheese and smoked-turkey luncheon meat between rye crackers.

6. Quick Pizza Snack: Split English muffins and spread with 2 table-spoons of your favorite Italian tomato sauce. Cover muffins with pepperoni slices and sprinkle on grated mozzarella cheese. Broil pizzas until the cheese melts, 3 to 5 minutes or about 1 minute in the microwave.

7. Taco Dip: Mix 2 tablespoons of taco seasoning with 1 cup sour cream. This makes a great dip for crackers, chips, carrot and celery sticks, cucumbers and green pepper slices.

8. Quesadillas: In a lightly-oiled frying pan, sprinkle 1/4 cup shredded cheddar cheese on a flour tortilla. Add 1 teaspoon of chopped mild green chilies if you like a spicier flavor. Add a

layer of tortilla and cheese; top with a tortilla. Cover and cook on low to medium heat until the cheese melts, about 3 to 5 minutes. Remove quesadilla from the pan with a spatula, put four dollops of picante sauce and sour cream on top. Cut it in pie-shaped wedges and serve.

9. Little Smokies: Your hungry athletes will love these. Simmer a 1-pound package of little smokey sausages, 1 cup mustard and 1 cup plum jelly in a heavy skillet for 30 minutes. Spear sausages with toothpicks to eat.

10. Frozen Bananas: Cut bananas in half, insert an ice cream stick in the cut end of the banana. Put bananas on a tray or pan, and freeze; after frozen, store bananas in self-locking storage bags. When you're ready to eat them, allow bananas to thaw slightly. Dip into different toppings, such as coconut, flavored yogurt, finely chopped nuts or seeds or peanut butter.

11. Cheese Cookies: Mix 1/4 pound shredded cheddar cheese and 1/4 cup softened margarine until light and fluffy. Mix 1 cup white flour and 1/2 teaspoon salt and stir into cheese mixture. Chill dough for an hour. Heat oven to 350 degrees. Roll dough into balls the size of large walnuts. Place balls on baking sheet a few inches apart; flatten with a fork dipped in flour. Bake 12 to 15 minutes. Makes about 3 dozen.

12. Sausage Balls: Take 1/2 pound of sausage out of the refrigerator, and leave at room temperature for 30 minutes. Mix sausage, 1 cup grated cheddar cheese and 2 cups biscuit mix with your hands. Heat oven to 350 degrees. Shape in-

to balls the size of small walnuts. Place them a few inches apart on an ungreased baking sheet. Bake 30 minutes. Makes about 4 dozen.

Sweet Treats

13. Banana Whip: Peel a banana, wrap it in plastic wrap, and freeze. Blend frozen banana with 1/2 cup of half-and-half, 2 tablespoons honey and 1 teaspoon vanilla in a blender on high speed until smooth.

14. Spread peanut butter on graham crackers. Make funny faces with raisins or chocolate chips. You can also stuff a cored apple with a mixture of peanut butter and raisins or chocolate chips.

15. Dip bananas or apple slices in warmed caramel ice cream topping. Try apple slices, banana pieces, pineapple chunks or fresh strawberries dipped in powdered cherry or strawberry gelatin.

16. Easy Orange Delight: Combine a 6-ounce can frozen orange juice concentrate with 1 cup water, 1 cup milk, 1/4 cup sugar, 1 teaspoon vanilla and 1 cup ice cubes in a blender. Blend until smooth and frothy and ice cubes are chopped up.

17. Mountain Trail Mix: Mix 1 cup raisins, 1/2 cup dried banana chips, 1 cup of your favorite nuts and 1 cup chocolate-coated candies. Store trail mix in a self-locking plastic bag.

18. Mystery Chocolate Munchies: In the top of a double boiler, melt a 12-ounce package of semi-sweet chocolate chips over low heat. Stir in 6

ounces chow mein noodles until they are evenly coated. Drop teaspoonfuls on a baking sheet covered with waxed paper. Put in the refrigerator. Let set for about 10 to 15 minutes. For variation, use butterscotch chips.

19. Quick Cinnamon Doughnuts: Combine 1 cup granulated sugar and 1 tablespoon cinnamon in a shallow bowl or pie pan. Add an inch or two of cooking oil to a large frying pan, and heat until oil reaches 375 degrees. Punch large holes in the centers of refrigerated biscuits with your finger. Carefully drop about five doughnuts into the hot oil. Keep turning them until they are golden brown. Remove doughnuts from the oil and drain on paper towels for a few seconds. Roll warm doughnuts in the cinnamon and sugar.

20. Pudding Cones: Prepare 1 package of your favorite instant pudding. Fill flat-bottomed ice cream cones with pudding. Top with candy sprinkles or miniature marshmallows, if desired. Eat immediately; don't store in the refrigerator because the cone will collapse.

21. Chocolate Mint Cookies: Melt a 12-ounce package of semi-sweet chocolate chips in a double boiler over barely simmering water. Remove pan from the stove. Mix 1 teaspoon of peppermint extract and 2 teaspoons of vegetable oil into the melted chips. Dip Ritz Crackers into the warm chocolate. Put the crackers on waxed paper until they are set, and then store in a covered container in the refrigerator. Makes about 3 dozen chocolate crackers. Variation: Leave out the peppermint extract, spread peanut butter between two crackers and dip them in the melted chocolate.

Chapter 9

Enhancing Your Child's Education

School deadlines tend to incite chaos at our homes. One night at the Mahaffey house, Joy and Mark were busily helping Kristi and Mac with important assignments. At the same time, Bill, their third child, decided to invent slime in the kitchen. Because he used too much baking soda, vinegar and yeast, the slime grew all over the countertop and ran down the cabinets. By then Bill had left to do another project, but John Mark, his preschool brother, discovered this intriguing concoction. He had eaten some of it and had started smearing it all over himself and the floor when Joy found him.

Although helping our kids with school projects often stretches our patience out of shape, we feel it's important to be involved in their educational development. Teachers at various grade levels we surveyed agreed that children receive an above-average education when their parents take an active role.

"Déjá vague—the feeling you get when your child asks about a math problem that you didn't understand at his age, much less now."

So many a week night, you'll find us calling out spelling words, helping with a science project, listening to an oral book report or fitting a costume for a school play—even though the recliner and evening paper look enticing.

The following ideas offer many ways you can help your children develop skills based on their learning style. (See the special Learning Styles guide on page 57.)

Younger Children

1. Read to young children daily. This helps them develop listening and observation skills and stimulates imagination. Let your child read to you and point out the pictures. Preschoolers enjoy pretending to read the story.

2. Teach young children how to follow directions; it is one of the most important skills they need in school. When showing children how to perform a new task or skill, model each part of

the job. Then let them participate with you until they can do the task alone. Give instructions one at a time, followed by doing that part of the task. Too many directions at the same time confuse children.

3. When you take preschool children to the bank, bakery, cleaners, post office or service station, tell them about the kinds of work the people do and why their services are needed.

4. Listen to sounds with your child, and talk about what you hear: workers repairing the street, a train whistle, dogs barking, cash register ringing or birds chirping. For fun, try to mimic the sounds together.

5. Young children need to build with blocks, play with clay, put together puzzles and do simple exercises, such as bending, crawling, hopping, stretching or walking. This helps them develop their large and small motor skills and prepares them to learn tasks that require physical dexterity at school.

6. Before reading a new book to young children, tell them the title and ask what they think the story might be about. When you have almost finished reading the book, ask your children to make up an ending to the story.

7. Link reading books with television programs. If your child watches a show about birds, check out a book at the library on the same subject, and read it together.

Older Kids

8. Show interest in your child's school work, and display it on a bulletin board. Look at their textbooks, and ask them what they enjoy learning about the most. Ask them what subjects are difficult for them and where they need help.

9. Set up a good study environment. Some children like to be alone and quiet, while others prefer to be near people. Our children study at the kitchen or dining room table. We keep a basket of school supplies for homework projects, such as construction, lined and plain white paper; different colors of felt pens and pencils; folders for reports; and poster board.

10. Encourage children to read for pleasure and always have a book "in process." Praise them regularly, and show interest in what they're reading by asking questions about the story and the characters.

11. Play Quartermania, a game devised to cut down on TV viewing and to encourage more creative pursuits. The object is to move all the quarters (between fifteen and twenty dollars) from jar A to jar B. When jar B is full, then the children can buy a predetermined item. Children can earn one quarter for reading for thirty minutes from a good book; one for great manners; one for watching an hour of TV a day; two for watching thirty minutes of TV; and three for watching no TV. Parents can take a quarter out of jar B and put it back in jar A for bad attitudes or bad table manners.

12. Create homework incentive programs. (See our Homework Contract on page 58.) Children earn points toward an award by doing homework on the day that it is assigned, completing it on

time and having a good attitude.

13. Study along with your kids. One mom enrolled in an algebra refresher course at the local college so that she could help her freshman son with his studies.

14. Stress the importance of neatness. Teachers are influenced by the way work looks. If your children's handwriting is poor, encourage them to do the best they can. When possible, let your children do their work on a computer or a typewriter. Two of the most important classes your child may take will be typing and word processing.

15. Keep a good dictionary and synonym finder handy. When your children read a word they don't know or hear an unfamiliar word on TV, teach them to look it up.

16. Build your vocabulary as a family; learn a new word every morning at the breakfast table. You can buy daily calendars with unusual or unfamiliar words; they also give the definition, a pronunciation guide and a sentence to show how the word is used. They have versions of these word calendars for older and younger children. Kathy realized a little word learning must be sinking in and had to smile when one of her boys said, "Mom, I'll be sitting behind the octogenarian with psilosis." He was simply saying, "I'll be sitting behind the eighty-year-old, bald-headed man."

17. Help your children learn to study effectively for tests:

A. Review notes soon after class.

B. Color-code essential information with a highlight pen in textbooks (if they own them). It also helps to highlight class notes. This makes it easier to review the important points.

C. Ask the teacher what a test will cover, if they're unsure about it.

D. Save old tests; they make great study guides.

E. Study with several other students to review material before a test.

F. Study according to their biological clock. When is their best time, early morning or evening?

G. Commit information to memory only when they're rested.

H. Learn how to use memory strategies, such as acronyms, key words, linking ideas and rhyming.

I. Proofread papers before handing them in, and use a spelling dictionary as a quick way to check words for errors.

18. Discuss how to do special projects or papers with your children before they start them. Help your children think through the following questions: What does the teacher want? What items do you need to complete the project? What is available? What other resources do you need to check into?

19. See what resources are available before starting projects and reports. Your public library often houses special collections in various subjects. It may also carry clippings or memorabilia on local history. Grandparents may have an antique, old books, newspapers or photographs that could be used for an interesting report. One boy had to do

a paper on the judicial system, and he interviewed a friend of the family, who is a judge. If you have a hobby, your child can often use it as a source for a project.

20. A cassette tape player is a great learning tool for children who are auditory learners or who have difficulty reading. Here are some ways a recorder can be used:

A. Have your child record his or her report before writing it. Then listen to the tape, and take down the report on paper.

B. Record reading assignments for your children, such as a story or a chapter from a textbook. They can listen to the recording and follow along in the book. This way your children can check what they're hearing against what's being read. They can listen to the recording several times to reinforce learning and improve reading skills.

C. Ask the teacher for permission to use a tape recorder in class. Many children find it helpful to hear the lecture and assignment more than once.

D. Encourage children who don't enjoy reading or don't read well to listen to stories on tape. Many local libraries offer tapes of classical literature as well as fun stories for young children.

21. Help your child learn handy skills. Repair a bike, take apart a small appliance, or build a simple piece of furniture together.

22. Enroll your children in enrichment classes such as art, dance, drama, music or science. These courses are often available for free or for a nominal fee through city parks and recreation departments, junior colleges and YMCAs.

23. Take your child to programs that complement a subject he or she is studying in school. For example, a civic theater, high school or college may present a play or a musical your child is learning about in class. A planetarium may offer a course about the moon, which will make science studies come alive.

24. Engage in stimulating discussions at the dinner table. Leo Buscaglia's father insisted that each child learn at least one new thing every day to share at dinner. No piece of information was too small or unimportant to be discussed at their dinner table.[1]

1. Leo Buscaglia, "Our Dinner Table University," *Reader's Digest,* September 1989, 78-80.

Learning Styles

A key element in helping your child is to understand his or her learning style, which can be auditory, visual and/or kinesthetic. Discovering your children's learning styles will help prevent unnecessary frustration for them and you.

After calling out spelling words to one of her sons for the fifth time, Joy realized that vocal cues would not work because he was not an auditory learner. He was a visual and kinesthetic learner. It worked well for him to use the letters from a Scrabble game to practice his spelling words. Another son was stumped memorizing the capitals and countries in Europe. He traced, color-coded and numbered a map. When he finished making the study sheet, he had learned fifteen of the thirty capitals. Another son, however, needed auditory cues and learned his alphabet easier when Joy sang the alphabet song with him.

A child will transfer from one style to another when the need arises. But one or two of these learning styles will predominate throughout a child's lifetime.

You can determine a lot about your children's learning style by watching them. Listen to the words they use: Do they talk about what they see (visual) or hear (auditory)? Or do they say, "Show me" (kinesthetic)? Observe your children while they play. Do they watch or read to acquire information, listen intently or want to do it with their hands? By the time children are four or five, you can ask them how they would prefer to learn, and they can tell you.

Auditory learners like to sit where they can hear well. They need to talk about what they hear. They may not appear to be watching what is going on in the classroom, but they are listening. They gain information through sound, so they read aloud to themselves or silently mouth the words. Auditory learners talk to themselves and others when they're bored. They recall names better than faces, and they may have difficulty with conceptual subjects such as math. They learn in a noisy atmosphere better than visual learners, who prefer quiet surroundings.

Visual learners sit in front of the classroom so they can see what is going on. They talk about what they see. They learn better by reading than by listening. They make mental pictures of what they read or hear. They need to write information down and take detailed notes. They like colorful illustrations and lots of pictures. They prefer to watch something when they are bored, and they remember faces better than names.

Kinesthetic learners need hands-on experiences. They like to feel things and communicate by touching. They often say, "Show me how to do it." They use their hands to gesture when they talk. When they feel confined, they move around, or when they're bored, they fiddle with an object, such as twirling a pencil. They prefer field trips or being outdoors over classroom activities.

Once you help your children understand their learning styles, school will become more rewarding.

Homework Contract

Week of _Oct. 21_

Name _Timothy_

	Monday	Tuesday	Wednesday	Thursday	Friday	Weekend
Studies Completed: Yes or No	yes	yes	no	yes	yes	no
Completed on Time: Yes or No	5:00 yes	7:00 yes	5:00 no	7:00 no	5:00 yes	saturday 6:00 no
Attitude **Poor** 1 2 **Fair** 3 4 **Good** 5	1 2 3 4 (5)	1 2 3 (4) 5	1 (2) 3 4 5	1 2 3 4 (5)	1 2 (3) 4 5	1 (2) 3 4 5

I agree to do my homework with a good attitude every day that it is assigned.

_____Timothy_____
(child's signature)

I agree to reward _____Timothy_____ with _one pack of base ball cards_, if
(child's name)   (specify reward)

homework is completed every day this week by the agreed time, and if ___20___
(number)

points have been earned for a good attitude.

_____Janet Evans_____
(parent's signature)

Homework Contract

Week of _____

Name _____

	Monday	Tuesday	Wednesday	Thursday	Friday	Weekend
Studies Completed: Yes or No						
Completed on Time: Yes or No						
Attitude						
Poor	1	1	1	1	1	1
	2	2	2	2	2	2
Fair	3	3	3	3	3	3
	4	4	4	4	4	4
Good	5	5	5	5	5	5

I agree to do my homework with a good attitude every day that it is assigned.

_____
  (child's signature)

I agree to reward _____ with _____ , if
                                    (child's name)   (specify reward)

homework is completed every day this week by the agreed time, and if _____
                                                                                                          (number)

points have been earned for a good attitude.

_____
  (parent's signature)

Chapter 10

Increasing Your Child's Creativity Quotient

Many children discover their life's work through creative, playful activities. As parents of future Thomas Edisons, this means we need to give up our dreams of winning the House Beautiful award. Inventive pursuits often produce creative messes. At our homes, we sometimes have artistic creations and contraptions covering every countertop and table, not to mention the latest thingamajig hanging from the ceiling. Some days we feel like putting a sign on our front door, announcing: Future entrepreneurs at work. Enter at your own risk!

Here are some ideas to foster creativity:

1. As a family, read aloud inspirational stories and biographies of inventors or courageous people who have hurdled over huge problems or handicaps. Discuss how the people met challenges creatively and overcame their difficulties.

"A person might be able to play without being creative, but he (or she) sure can't be creative without playing."

Kurt Hanks and Jay A. Parry

2. When your children want to experiment with creative enterprises or have invented a new way to do a project, encourage them to try it. Eleven-year-old Bill Mahaffey noticed that a young friend needed to have his wheelchair pushed over door thresholds. As a result, Bill is designing a portable ramp that attaches to the wheelchair, so that his friend can maneuver over obstacles by himself.

3. Provide your children with the opportunity to do creative projects they show interest in, such as drawing, gardening, sewing, building models, caring for animals, cross stitching, computer programming, investigating nature, collecting rocks, learning simple geology or working on mechanical projects.

4. Encourage activities that stimulate imagina-

tion and resourcefulness. One day Kathy's kids created lost in outer space survival kits. They used old backpacks, paper towel rolls, handles from broken ski poles, and ice cream sticks to make survival gear and tools.

5. Help your children think of imaginative ways to do projects. When Kathy's son ran for a class office, the family brainstormed campaign strategies and how he could use the name "Peel": John, an A–PEELING PRES. Don't Slip Up, Vote for the Peel—on a banana-shaped poster, of course! Even though the race was lost, the posters still remind the family of the fun time they had together.

6. If there is something your older children want to do or buy, help them think of creative ways to earn some or all the money. They will value it more if they have worked for it. Our children have baby-sat, mowed lawns, sold registered dogs and started their own spring flower-bulb business.

7. Renovate an old toy or game, or build your own. We restored an old bicycle, invented a new batting tee when the old one fell apart and built a space station pad from scrap lumber.

The oldest two Peel boys asked if they could build a racetrack for their youngest brother's small cars. They were sure the track would be superior and less expensive than one the Peels could buy. Kathy was tempted to say no, but she let them construct the hardboard, plexiglass racetrack. Now it is the envy of every child in the neighborhood.

8. Around the dinner table, imagine ways that an ordinary object could be used. For example, a facial tissue could be made into a parachute for a toy, a bedspread for a doll, or wadded up it could make a ball for a game, or folded it could make a bandage. What could you create from the following objects: a ball point pen, paper clip, spoon or soup can?

9. Play Twenty Questions.[1] Choose one person to be it. He or she thinks of a person, place or thing and gives a clue about what it might be. For example, "I am a thing. I am always hot." The first player either tries to guess or says, "I don't know." If the first player doesn't know the correct answer, then a different clue is given to the next player. Clues could be, "I can be up or down." "I am a favorite at the beach." "I can have spots." Keep going around the circle giving clues until someone guesses the answer—which in this case is the sun. The person who guesses correctly becomes the one to give the clues. Keep score; the one with the most correct answers wins the game. This guessing game stimulates creative thinking because it makes you put aside preconceived ideas of what the answer should be and provokes you to think about alternatives.

The Peels also created a preschool version of Twenty Questions for their youngest son. This is fun to play in the car or while you're waiting for an appointment. Mom or dad asks the child simple questions about familiar persons, places or things. For example, clues might be: "I am an animal." "I have four legs." "I just had eleven babies." The child continues guessing until he or she says the right answer, which is: "It's my dog, Honey!"

10. Make up stories that stimulate your children's imagination. They will enjoy animal adventures or ones where they are the main characters. At bedtime, Kathy tells her five-year-old son tales of Banjo and Missy, two dogs who run away from home. She stops at a high point, so her son will anticipate the following night's episode. He usually begs: "Please tell me what happens next!"

11. Tell a continuing story. It can be an exciting drama or a hilarious comedy. This is a fun activity to do in the car or around the dinner table. One family member starts the story, and each person after that adds more to the adventure. For example,

Dad: There once was a dog named Charlie who lived . . .

Mom: . . . in a small town in Colorado. He was a medium-sized dog. . .

Child One: . . . with black and white spots. Everyone loved Charlie in the town because . . .

Child Two: . . . he had rescued many people who had fallen into snow drifts that winter. But one afternoon . . . .

1. This has been adapted from the board game Twenty Questions, University Games/Scott A. Mednick, 1987.

Chapter 11

Making the Most of Magazines

When kids start school, it doesn't take long for parents to learn the importance of collecting good magazines. Magazines can be used to help preschoolers learn the alphabet and phonics; elementary-age children increase reading and learning skills; and high schoolers study current events and trends. We have spent many a night helping our children find pictures of animals, products of a foreign country or examples of metaphors and similes in the stories. Children's magazines also include creative projects and unique games and puzzles.

The following ideas offer ways to make the most of magazines:

Younger Children

1. Help young children develop observation and language skills by identifying colors and finding and naming pictures of animals, fruits, people, toys or other objects in magazines. This is a good

"It's amazing how interesting old magazines become once you've resolved to clear them out of the basement."

Burton Hillis

activity to do while waiting in the doctor's office.

2. Teach children letters of the alphabet. Look for all the "A's" or "B's" on a magazine page. As the child finds the letter, he or she can color it with a highlight pen.

3. Make an alphabet book. In a spiral notebook, write each letter of the alphabet on different pages. Look through magazines, and help your child find pictures that begin with each letter. Cut out the pictures and paste them in the notebook.

4. Kindergartners enjoy cutting pictures out of magazines, gluing them into a spiral notebook and making up a story about the illustrations. Have them dictate their story to you, then write it for them next to each picture.

Older Children

5. Keep files of newspaper and magazine

articles and pictures your child might need for future projects. Files could include pictures of animals, foods, people, places or various modes of transportation. The following kinds of articles and stories will be useful: arts and crafts, historical, scientific, technical or accounts of modern-day heroes or heroines. Humorous anecdotes, interesting quotations or statistics, recipes or scientific discoveries will also come in handy.

6. Set up a magazine reading incentive program. For every article or story children read, they can earn points toward a certain prize. Have them write down the title of the piece, one sentence telling what the piece was about, or state three important points. This helps children clarify what they have read and helps the parent see how much the children understand.

7. If your children have difficulty reading or don't enjoy books, encourage them to read short articles and stories in magazines designed for their age group. Colorful illustrations and larger print give children the feeling that the pieces will be easier to read.

8. Have poor readers read aloud brief stories from magazines for practice. They will feel successful if they can finish a story in a short time.

9. Ask your child to color highlight all the words he or she doesn't recognize in a story. Go over the words, pronounce them, and help your child look up definitions. Use the words in other sentences.

10. Help your children see that they are improving in their reading ability. Have them read a magazine story at their reading level, color highlighting the words they know. In a couple of weeks, have your children read the story again and mark words they recognize now.

11. Have your child read magazine advertisements and circle the adjectives. Discuss how these descriptive words influence our decision to purchase products.

12. Collect illustrations from magazines that budding artists can try to copy.

13. Help your child submit pictures, poems, riddles or stories to children's magazines. They could be published!

14. Cut out individual letters, phrases or words from magazines, and glue them onto paper, making an anonymous note to a friend.

15. Let your children relax before they go to sleep by reading magazines in bed.

16. Magazine Treasure Hunt: Give each child an old magazine with pictures. List twenty-five things to hunt for, such as a boy, girl, car, flowers or horse. Have the children tear the items out of the magazine and put them in a paper bag. Allow twenty minutes to find all the items. The one with the most treasures wins. It's also fun to divide into four or five teams, but set the time limit for ten minutes.

17. Make a zany personal collage. Cut out a face and neck from an old school picture. Find another

picture in a magazine for the body. A boy might choose an athlete or a muscle builder's body. Glue the picture of the face with the body on poster board. Cut out more magazine pictures, positive descriptive words or phrases, and cover the entire poster board with them. Pictures of favorite hobbies or interests could also be used. This collage is also fun to do for a friend on his or her birthday.

18. Create games using pictures from magazines. We created Name That Song and Name That Bible Character. We cut out pictures for clues and glue them on construction paper. The pictures represent a letter, syllable or word. For example, one page of clues has the letter J, a plus sign and a picture of corn on the cob. The answer for this one is Jacob. Another clue shows a picture of a piece of pie, a plus sign and a parking lot. The answer to this set of clues is Pilate.

Magazines for Kids of all Ages

Collect, check out from the library or subscribe to magazines that appeal to your children. We've listed a few periodicals they might enjoy:*

1. *Air & Space/Smithsonian Magazine,* Smithsonian, 900 Jefferson Drive, Washington, D.C. 20560.

2. *Boys' Life,* Boy Scouts of America, 1325 Walnut Hill Lane, Irving, Texas 75028-3096 (ages 8-18).

3. *Breakaway,* Focus on the Family, Pomona, California 91799 (guys, teens).

4. *Brio,* Focus on the Family, Pomona, California 91799, (gals, teens).

5. *Chickadee Magazine,* Young Naturalist Foundation, 56 The Esplanade, Suite 306, Toronto, Ontario M5E 1A7, Canada (ages 4-9).

6. *Clubhouse,* Focus on the Family, Pomona, California 91799 (ages 8-12).

7. *Clubhouse Jr.,* Focus on the Family, Pomona, California 91799 (ages 4-7).

8. *Highlights for Children,* 803 Church Street, Honesdale, Pennsylvania 18431 (ages 2-12).

9. *Humpty Dumpty,* Children's Better Health Institute, 1100 Waterway Boulevard, P.O. Box 567, Indianapolis, Indiana 46206 (ages 4-6).

10. *Kid City*™, Children's Television Workshop, 1 Lincoln Plaza, New York, New York 10023 (ages 6-10).

11. *National Geographic World,* National Geographical Society, P.O. Box 2330, Washington, D.C. 20012-9865 (ages 8-12).

12. *Owl Magazine: The Discovery Magazine for Children,* The Young Naturalist Foundation, 56 The Esplanade, Suite 306, Toronto, Ontario, M5E 1A7, Canada.

13. *Pack-O-Fun,* 14 Main Street, Park Ridge, Illinois 60068 (ages 5-9).

14. *Popular Science,* 2 Park Avenue, New York, New York 10016.

15. *Ranger Rick,* National Wildlife Federation, 1412 Sixteenth Street, NW, Washington, D.C. 20036 (ages 6-12).

16. *Reader's Digest,* Pleasantville, New York 10570.

17. *Sports Illustrated for Kids,* P.O. Box 830609, Birmingham, Alabama 35283-0609.

18. *3-2-1 Contact,* Children's Television Workshop, 1 Lincoln Plaza, New York, New York 10023 (ages 8-14).

19. *Your Big Backyard,* National Wildlife Federation, 1412 Sixteenth Street, NW, Washington, D.C. 20036 (ages 3-5).

20. *Youthwalk,* Focus on the Family, Pomona, California 91799 (high school).

*Some of the secular magazines may periodically include articles that reflect views other than your own.

Chapter 12

Science Fair? Don't Despair

"Mom, my science fair project is due tomorrow," your child suddenly remembers as you tuck him into bed.

Your blood pressure rises, your smile turns into a frown, and your stomach flip-flops. What's a parent to do?! For those panic moments, we've listed a few easy science fair projects. These experiments contain three basic elements—the problem, the procedure and the results or conclusion. Your school may require a variation of these components.

Some of the periodicals mentioned in "Making the Most of Magazines" also carry science articles, projects and pictures for reports. To avoid future heart-pounding moments, keep a file of science fair ideas.

Have your children try these experiments at home before doing them in front of a classroom to spare an embarrassing disaster:

"Question on a science test: 'In what three states does water exist?' Student blurts out: 'All 50!'"

M.S.G.

Younger Children

1. *Problem:* What conducts sound better, air or water?

Method: Fill a balloon with water and tie a knot in its neck. Hold a ticking watch on one side of the balloon, press your ear to the opposite side of the balloon, and listen to the sound. Now listen to the watch without the balloon. Can you hear the ticking equally well both ways, or is one way louder than the other?

Result: The ticking is louder when you press your ear to the balloon, so water conducts sound better than air.

2. *Problem:* Does sound travel better through air or solid materials?

Method: Make a tin can telephone. Remove the top lid of two soup cans. Use a small nail to punch a hole in the bottom lid at the center of each can. Thread one end of heavy string, twenty feet in length, through the hole of one can and tie a knot inside the can. Thread the other end of the string through the hole in the second can from the outside. Tie a knot in the end of the string, so it won't slip out of the hole. One child takes one can and walks away from the second child who holds the other can. Stretch the string taut. The first child says a simple sentence in a low voice into the can while the second child holds the open side of the other can to his or her ear and listens. Then the first child says the same sentence in a low voice from the same distance but without the tin can telephone receiver.

Result: Sound travels better and faster through solids than through air. When you speak into the can, vibrations carry the sound through the air into the can and down the string to the second can. (Vibrations are quivering motion.)[1]

3. *Problem:* How do you produce static electricity?

Method: Blow up a balloon, and tie its neck in a knot. Rub the balloon against a piece of woolen material. Then place the balloon about two or three inches away from your hair.

Result: Static produces electrical disturbances. The friction from the balloon rubbing against the woolen material causes free electrons to leave the cloth and attach to the balloon, giving it a negative charge. The free electrons are repelled by the hair, giving the hair a positive charge. Hair stands up and is drawn toward the balloon because opposites attract. (This experiment works best on cold, dry days.)[2]

4. *Problem:* Does air take up space?

Method: Pack a paper napkin tightly into the bottom of an eight-ounce canning jar or a clear glass. Hold the glass straight, and lower it open side down into a large mixing bowl half-filled with water. Observe how much water goes into the glass. Now tip the glass slightly.

Result: Air takes up space because air has density. When the glass is held straight, water compresses the air, squeezing it together and reducing it in volume. The air is pushed into the glass, preventing the water from filling it and getting the napkin wet. When the glass is tipped, the air escapes and it fills with water.[3]

5. *Problem:* How does atmospheric pressure work?

Method: Put a cup of water in a drinking glass. Suck enough water from the glass into a plastic straw to fill it up. Pinch the end of the straw tightly, and pull it completely out of the water. Now stop pinching the straw, and the water will drain back into the glass.

Result: Air creates pressure in all directions. Water stays in the plastic straw because your finger cuts off the air pressure. At the bottom of the straw, air presses against the water and keeps it from draining out. When you stop pinching the straw, air pressing from the top and bottom pushes with the same pressure, but gravity pulls the water downward to the earth.[4]

6. *Problem:* How is sound made?

Method: Hold one end of a wooden ruler firmly on a wood table or desk so that most of the ruler sticks out beyond the edge. With your free hand, quickly snap the end of the ruler downward several times. Listen for the sound. Now extend only half the ruler beyond the edge, and snap it again. Listen to the difference in the sound.

Result: The sound is made by the vibrations of the ruler, causing the air to vibrate and make sound. When the longer ruler is snapped, it vibrates more slowly and produces a lower-pitched sound. The shorter ruler vibrates faster and produces a higher pitch.[5]

Older Children

7. *Problem:* Demonstrate the attraction and the repulsion of objects when the surface tension of water is weakened by another substance.

Method: Break two toothpicks into eight pieces and float them in the center of a bowl half-filled with water. Hold a sugar cube in the water (don't let go of it), and watch the toothpicks. Remove the sugar cube before it dissolves. Dump the water, and put fresh water in the bowl. Cut a soap bar the size of a sugar cube. Put the toothpicks in the center of the bowl, and hold the soap in the water. Watch the toothpicks, and see what happens.

Result: The sugar cube is porous and attracts the toothpick pieces. The soap's oily film spreads out and repels the toothpicks. The surface of the water acts as if a thin, elastic film covers it. This surface is weakened when tension is created by substances that attract or repel.[6]

8. *Problem:* Does the force of magnetic attraction travel through water?

Method: Use masking tape to attach a small iron nail sideways to the bottom of a small plastic boat or to one side of a lightweight piece of scrap lumber that will float. Prop an aluminum cake pan on two bricks or boards so you can easily slip your hand underneath it. Fill the pan half full with water, and float the boat in it. Hold a magnet against the bottom of the pan under the boat and move it around; watch the boat follow the magnet.

Result: The magnetic force travels through water and attracts the iron nail.[7]

9. *Problem:* Does air have weight?

Method: Blow up two balloons the same size. Tie a small piece of string around the neck of the balloons, then tie them to opposite ends of a yardstick. Tie a string to the middle of the stick, and suspend it from a door frame with a thumb tack or masking tape. Adjust the string and balloons at each end of the stick, so they are evenly balanced. Make sure the stick has stopped swinging, then pop one of the balloons with a pin.

Result: When both balloons are filled with air, it is compressed inside the balloons, and they both weigh the same. The end of the stick goes up when the balloon is popped because the compressed air has escaped. The balloon filled with compressed air pulls the stick down, which shows that air has weight.[8]

10. *Problem:* Does air exert pressure?

Method: (Blow up a balloon first and let the air out of it to make it easier to do this experiment.) Hold a balloon, putting the bottom part of it into a clear-glass pint jar. Blow up the balloon until it touches the sides of the glass. Keep blowing until you can lift the jar by holding the neck of the balloon closed.

Result: This shows how air exerts pressure. When the balloon expands against the sides of the jar, the pressure allows you to lift the balloon and the jar.[9]

11. *Problem:* What is the chemical reaction between white vinegar and baking soda?

Method: Fill a clear-glass quart jar with three cups of water; add one tablespoon of baking soda and three drops of food coloring. Stir well. Add one tablespoon of popcorn kernels and four tablespoons of white vinegar. Watch what happens to the kernels. When the kernels stop moving up and down, add one tablespoon of baking soda and one tablespoon of vinegar. Stir gently.

Result: Chemicals in the baking soda and white vinegar combine to form carbon dioxide bubbles. The bubbles attach to the popcorn kernels, causing them to float to the top. When the bubbles burst, the kernels sink.[10]

12. *Problem:* Does air have muscles?

Method: Using a rubber band or string, tie together three one-inch thick books, about seven-and-a-half-by-ten-inches, and lay them on top of a flattened balloon on the edge of a table. The mouthpiece of the balloon must hang over the edge. Slowly blow up the balloon. Watch what happens to the books.

Result: Air exerts pressure and lifts the books.[11]

13. *Problem:* How do you measure the dew point?

Method: Fill a coffee can with water. Hold an outdoor thermometer near the outside of the can, and check and record the temperature. This is the air temperature. Pour out half the water, gradually add three to four ice cubes, and stir with a spoon. Continue to add more ice cubes until dew forms on the outside of the can. As soon as the dew forms, hold the thermometer in the ice water, watch the temperature drop, and record it when it stays at one point.

Result: This is the dew point. Dew point is the temperature at which water condenses out of the air and forms droplets of water on the outside of the can. The dew point temperature is lower than the air temperature. (The dew point is not a fixed temperature, because it depends on the moisture content of the air.)[12]

14. *Problem:* How does a rocket engine work?

Method: Use a piece of sturdy fishing line about six feet long. Secure one end of the line to the top of a chair back, using masking tape. Thread the other end of the line through a drinking straw, attach it with masking tape to the top back of another chair, and pull the chairs apart so the line is taut. Move the straw so that one end is resting against the back of a chair. One child blows up an oblong balloon and holds the nozzle closed to keep air from escaping while placing the balloon under the straw. The nozzle of the balloon needs to be pointed toward the chair back. A second child attaches one strip of transparent tape to one side of the balloon, brings it over the straw, then sticks the tape to the other side of the balloon. Do the same with a second piece of tape. Let go of the nozzle and watch the balloon propel the straw toward the opposite chair.

Result: The balloon moves in the opposite direction of the escaping air, just like a jet moves in the opposite direction of its escaping fuel. This demonstrates Sir Isaac Newton's Third Law of Motion, which states that for every action or force, there is an equal and opposite reaction or force.[13]

15. *Problem:* Will salt melt ice?

Method: Put an ice cube in a small cereal bowl.

Add enough water to barely cover the ice cube. Moisten the end of a six-inch piece of kite string, and lay it on the ice. Sprinkle a spoonful of table salt over the string. Now gently pull up on the loose end of the string, and lift the ice cube.

Result: The salt melts the ice at first but loses heat during the process. Then the ice cube causes the salt water to re-freeze the end of the string to the cube.[14]

16. *Problem:* Are images reversed in a mirror?

Method: Stand a mirror upright, and put a piece of paper on a table in front of it. Look in the mirror, and write a short message that looks correct in the reflection. (This takes a lot of practice.)

Result: When you look at the paper without the mirror, the writing will be backwards. The mirror's surface reflects rays of light, which form an image on the retina of our eyes. This mirror image is always reversed. To read the message correctly hold it in front of the mirror.[15]

17. *Problem:* Can you see your pulse beat? Will your pulse rate go faster and slower, or does it stay the same?

Method: Break off the flammable head of a wooden match, so the remaining portion is about one-inch long. Push a flat-headed thumb tack into the end of the match. Lay one hand on the table palm side up; set the head of the thumbtack on the inside of your wrist and watch the movement of the match. Now run around the room a couple of times, and then put the head of the tack on your wrist again. Look how the match moves now.

Result: The pulse is the movement of your blood as it pumps from your heart through your arteries. You can see your pulse because the tack is near an artery on the inside of the wrist. When you're quiet, your pulse rate is slower than when you are active.[16]

18. *Problem:* What kind of glue can you make from milk and white vinegar?

Method: Pour two cups of skim milk and one cup of white vinegar into a small saucepan. Heat mixture over medium temperature about one minute or until it begins to boil, gently stirring with a spoon until it forms lumps. Remove pan from heat and pour lumpy mixture into a bowl. When it cools, pour the clear liquid off the top. Dissolve one teaspoon of baking soda in one-fourth cup of water, stir into the lumpy mixture until smooth. (This experiment smells terrible.)

Result: This shows the chemical interaction of milk when it is heated with vinegar. The acetic acid in the vinegar coagulates (thickens) the casein (a protein) in the skim milk and makes the lumps. The baking soda neutralizes the acid and forms a smooth glue. You can use this mixture to glue paper together.[17]

1. Martin L. Keen, *Let's Experiment* (New York: Grossett & Dunlap, Inc., 1968), 44.

2. Charles Vivian, *Science Experiments & Amusements for Children* (New York: Dover Publications, Inc., 1963), 26.

3. Vivian, *Science Experiments & Amusements,* 88.

4. Keen, *Let's Experiment,* 11.

5. Ibid., 42.

6. Vivian, *Science Experiments & Amusements,* 58.

7. Keen, *Let's Experiment,* 66.

8. Martin L. Keen, *Science Experiments* (New

York: Grossett & Dunlap, Inc., 1962), 10.

9. Vivian, *Science Experiments & Amusements*, 68.

10. Keen, *Let's Experiment*, 83.

11. Vivian, *Science Experiments & Amusements*, 22.

12. Keen, *Science Experiments*, 19.

13. Seymour Simon, *Science & Work* (New York: Franklin Watts, Inc., 1971), 54.

14. Vivian, *Science Experiments & Amusements*, 60.

15. Ibid., 84.

16. Ibid., 95.

17. Leonard de Vries, *The Third Book of Experiments* (New York: MacMillan Publishing Co., Inc., 1965), 22.

Chapter 13

An Apple for the Teacher

Parental involvement at school is an act of encouragement and support to the teacher. Plus it can make a difference not only for your child but also for the other children in the class. We have taken baskets of kittens and puppies, crawfish, lizards and quail eggs to our children's classes for science and pet care teaching units. The students had hands-on experience as we showed them how to feed, properly hold and take care of pets. Our children also enjoy taking us to school for show and tell. We usually read a favorite storybook to the students during this time.

Another way to foster a sense of your involvement in your child's schoolday experiences is to encourage your children to say thank you to their teachers. A phone call, short note or small gift says a lot.

In the listing below, we've suggested gift ideas that can be made by teens and elementary-age children; young children will need parental help.

"School teachers are not fully appreciated by parents until it rains all day Saturday."

We've also included ways for you to become more personally involved:

School Participation

1. Help with phone calls to organize classroom events or school fund-raisers. If you don't have time to bake, send napkins and plates for a school party.

2. When Joy had a baby and could not help at school, she graded papers at home. Her son Mac was proud to bring the papers to Mom after school.

3. Volunteer to help with an educational program. Joy helps coordinate an art program, involving 125 parents, for the local elementary school. Parents help teachers with creative projects and teach children the elements of art, such as line, shape, form and color design. Another mom is a cheerleading instructor. Schools often need help with computer programs, reading contests and the library.

4. Share your professional or specialized skills with a class. A carpenter could demonstrate the correct and safe way to use tools. A doctor might come when the class is studying the respiratory system during a science unit. A speech pathologist could give a lesson on how we hear. Let your child's teacher know that you are willing to talk to the class about a topic.

5. Hold a kite-flying-and-picnic day at your child's school.

6. Have a field day and picnic for the whole school. Memorial Day is a good time to schedule this event, since it's a holiday for many parents. Include relays, a football toss and a tug-of-war. Before the event, parents can help each class design its own T-shirt to wear for field day.

7. Sponsor an Invention Convention. Children are encouraged to invent a new product or a variation on an old one. They can sell or take orders for their inventions the day they're displayed. For example, an elementary-age girl's hair kept getting caught in the back of the chair when she worked at her desk. She made a fabric cover with ties for the chair back; she also included a pocket for books and supplies. Don't be surprised if you get some really creative inventions. A local TV station may be willing to cover this interesting event.

Fund Raisers

8. Help raise funds for special projects, such as computer equipment, educational events, field trips or library books. Organize a school carnival with game booths and bake sale items.

9. Hold a hot dog supper at the school for families.

10. Have an old-fashioned can or paper drive.

11. Around Christmas, hold a Saturday boutique, selling simple gifts and decorations that parents and students have made. This is also a good way to give kids a chance to buy inexpensive gifts for parents and siblings.

12. Pennies by the pound is a great fund-raiser for any school. Provide each class with a jar to collect pennies. The children may earn pennies for chores at home or ask parents and grandparents for them. Every day for a week, the pennies are weighed on a scale, and the weight is recorded on a chart. The class whose pennies weigh the most wins. Honor the winning class with a pizza party.

Teacher Appreciation Gifts

13. During the summer, make jams, jellies or relishes to be given as gifts to teachers during the school year.

14. Check with a local delicatessen or restaurant about purchasing a gift certificate for a lunch or dessert.

15. Fill a coffee mug or decorative tin with small candies. Cover container with plastic wrap and tie it with a ribbon.

16. One teacher said her favorite gift was a sack of pecans a student had picked for her.

17. Paint a border on an inexpensive acrylic picture frame with acrylic paints. Your teacher can put her family's picture on her desk.

18. Collage Pencil Holder: Cut out kind, encouraging words from magazines, such as awesome, best, great or wonderful. Glue the words all over an empty, clean soup can; then cover it with clear contact paper.

19. Teacher's Emergency Kit: In a clear plastic box, put in colored markers, pencils and pens, paper clips, transparent tape, small stapler, self-stick note pads, thumbtacks and a candy bar.

20. Garlic Chives: Fill a festive holiday mug with good potting soil. Plant two or three cloves of garlic in the soil. Keep soil lightly damp. Growth should occur in seven to ten days. Give the garlic plant as a gift, with instructions that the chives (green stalks) can be snipped for salads. Cut chives very fine, and mix with 1/2 cup softened margarine for garlic butter.

21. Bird Feeder Wreath: Buy an eight-inch styrofoam wreath. Mix 1/2 cup peanut butter with 1/2 cup shortening in a bowl. Spread mixture on the front side of the wreath. Press sunflower and bird seeds into the peanut butter mixture. Tie a ribbon around the top of the wreath as a hanger. Wrap the wreath in colored cellophane paper.

22. Herb Basket: Buy several potted herb seedlings from a nursery. Rosemary, sage and thyme work well, since they're evergreens. Set the pots and a booklet on herb growing in a basket lined with colored cellophane gift paper.

23. Christmas Bread Ornaments: Combine 4 cups flour with 1 cup salt; add 1 1/2 cups water. Stir the mixture with a spoon until it starts to form a smooth dough. Knead dough about 5 minutes. To make ornaments, pinch off bits of dough and form shapes such as bears, Christmas trees, gingerbread people and snowmen, or roll out the dough and use cookie cutters. To make hair, push a piece of dough through a garlic press. Bake at 350 degrees for 45 minutes or until golden brown. Paint with acrylic paints, then spray with clear acrylic spray. On the back of the ornament, write the name of the student and the year.

24. Gardener's Basket: Purchase a few small evergreen plants, garden gloves, terra-cotta pots and a booklet on gardening. Make a tag that says: "Thank you for nurturing and cultivating my child's life."

25. Bath salts: Put 1 pound of epsom salts in a large container with a lid. Add 15 drops of food coloring, tighten the lid of the container and shake it until the salt is colored. Divide into small jars, add a few drops of perfume and close jars tightly. Let stand about three weeks before using. Makes about three, eight-ounce jars of bath salts.

26. Soap Balls: Mix 1 cup Ivory Snow, 1/3 cup water, 5 drops food coloring and 3 drops of perfume in a bowl. Press soap mixture together with your hands, and shape it into one- to two-inch balls. Allow soap balls to dry for two days or until firm. Line a plastic strawberry basket or small box with colored tissue paper and fill with the soap balls. (Recommended for hand washing only.)

27. Remember Me Ornaments: Punch a small hole into the top of a frozen juice can lid with a nail. (Don't use lids that need to be removed with a can opener.) Cut a school picture to fit inside the rim of the lid, making a hole in the top of the picture to match the one in the lid. Glue picture inside lid, trim the outer edge with Christmas ribbon or rickrack, and attach an ornament hanger or a loop of yarn through the hole. Stick a label on the back of the ornament with the child's name, age, grade and school year.

28. Narcissus Paperwhites: These flowers are easy to grow indoors during the cold winter months. Use a low, wide bowl with no drainage hole, and fill it with pebbles. Plant bulbs in the pebbles so that the pointed end is up and half the bulb is exposed. Fill bowl with just enough water to touch the bottom of the bulb. Keep the water level the same at all times. Place bowl in a lighted, warm location (about 65 degrees). If you plant the bulbs in the fall, they will bloom in about 4 to 6 weeks. Bulbs planted in the winter will bloom in 3 to 4 weeks.

29. Handprint Shirt: Surprise your teacher with a T-shirt or sweatshirt with the handprints of all the (elementary-age) kids in the class. Put a very thin layer of acrylic paint in a disposable pie pan. Have each child gently press his or her hand into the paint and then firmly place it onto the shirt. Wash hand immediately with soap and water. Write the child's name under his or her print. At the bottom of the shirt, put the school year. An apron with handprints makes a nice gift, too.

30. Dog Lover's Basket: Fill a basket with homemade dog biscuits, a copy of the recipe, a colorful bandanna for the dog's neck and a cute thank-you card with a dog's picture on it.

Homemade Dog Biscuits
1 3/4 cups whole-wheat flour
1/2 cup cornmeal
1/2 cup instant oats
1/4 cup rye kernels
1/2 teaspoon salt
3 tbsp. liver powder
1/2 cup meat drippings or butter
1 egg
1/2 cup beef or chicken stock

Heat oven to 350 degrees. Stir dry ingredients together in a bowl. Cut in meat drippings or butter until the mixture resembles oatmeal. Mix in the egg, lightly beaten, and enough of the beef or chicken stock to form a ball. Knead the dough for a minute and roll it out on a floured board to about 1/4 inch thick. Cut dough with bone-shaped cookie cutters (check kitchen supply stores) or form your own. Prick each bone with a fork across the middle. Place the bones on an ungreased cookie sheet and bake for 25 to 30 minutes until brown. Cool on a wire rack. (Liver powder and rye kernels are available at health food stores.)

31. Spiced Tea Mix: This delightful tea mix will warm any teacher's heart. Pour the tea in jelly jars or self-closing storage bags, adding the directions, a pretty bow and card.

Spiced Tea Mix
2 cups Tang
1 1/2 cups sugar

1/2 cup unsweetened regular instant tea
1 package (0.14 oz.) lemon-flavored Kool-aid
1/2 tsp. ground cloves
1 tsp. ground cinnamon

Stir all the above ingredients in a bowl until thoroughly blended. To brew, add 2 teaspoons of the mix to a cup of hot water.

32. Easy Chili Dinner: This is a quick meal to fix at the end of a long day. In a colorful gift sack we include the recipe and spices for Bill's Famous Chili Mix, a package of commercial cornbread mix and Bill's Texas Pralines for dessert. Mix the spices in a bowl, and put them in a self-locking storage bag.

Bill's Famous Chili
1 lb. lean ground beef
1/2 cup chopped onion
3 tbsp. chili powder
1 tsp. cumin
1 tsp. oregano
1/2 tsp. garlic powder
1 tsp. salt
1/3 cup flour
1 (6 oz.) can of tomato paste

Brown ground beef and chopped onion; crumble meat with a fork. Stir in seasonings, flour, tomato paste and 4 cups water. Bring to a boil. Reduce heat and simmer for 30 minutes.

Bill's Texas Pralines
3/4 cup brown sugar
3/4 cup white sugar
1/2 cup evaporated milk
1 tbsp. butter (not margarine)
1/4 tsp. vanilla
1 cup pecan halves

Mix sugars and milk in a heavy 2-quart pan. Cook, stirring constantly, over low heat until sugars are dissolved. Cook over medium heat to soft ball stage (238 degrees). Remove from heat; stir in butter, vanilla and pecans. Beat until creamy. Stop beating when ripples show at edges of pan. Working quickly, drop teaspoonfuls on waxed paper, forming patties. Let stand until cool and set. Makes about 12 to 18 pralines.

33. One teacher told us that the best gift of all is when a former student returns to visit and expresses his or her appreciation. A thank-you is never too late.

Chapter 14

Inevitable Illnesses

During the school year, viruses rampage through our families, leaving rumpled beds and depleted energy in their wake. Isn't it amazing how, on the day a virus hits, that child has inevitably eaten chili, hot dogs or spaghetti for lunch? Once the stomach revenge strikes, you can count on it to pass through the family, one digestive system at a time.

Those anxious hours spent beside a child's sickbed or the tedious days enduring a lengthy siege of the chicken pox can be turned into warm, caring moments. Your children may remember, long after they're grown, the special care they received while they were sick.

The following activities will bring sunshine to those patients who are more sick of being stuck in the house than of being ill:

"The kids catch the flu in December, Sore throats come in March as a rule. Kids take their medicine cheerfully, As long as they get out of school."

Helpful Hints for Tender Loving Care

1. Most towns have the 911 emergency line, but it also helps to keep numbers handy for the ambulance, your doctor, the fire department, pharmacy or poison control hot line. When you have small children at home, a pharmacy that delivers is a tremendous help.

2. Keep a special shelf stocked with sick foods, such as chicken noodle soup, clear soda pop and soda crackers. Have necessary over-the-counter medications on hand, especially for unexpected bouts of the stomach flu. Children can become ill at very inconvenient hours!

3. Find out what your child prefers when he or she is sick. Some kids like to be left alone in their rooms; others want to be on the family room

sofa in the middle of things.

4. If your child is confined to bed and wants you nearby, do as many chores as you can in his or her room. Joy irons, folds laundry or cleans out closets and drawers in her patient's room.

5. Teach an older child to read a thermometer. The child can set a timer for the length of time the thermometer is supposed to remain under the tongue, and then record the temperature and time of day.

6. Create a pleasant atmosphere for your patients by giving them clean pillowcases and a fresh-cut flower by the bed or on the meal tray. Nice china, a pretty place mat and a cloth napkin make clear broth much nicer to drink.

7. At the Peel house, we have a large-size bib with the words "I Feel Better" painted on it. The bib comes in handy when the sick one is attempting to sip broth or eat a meal on a bed tray; besides it's fun to wear.

8. Make popsicles from fruit juice for a child with a sore throat.

9. Give good bland snacks like plain O-shaped cereals to a little one with a queasy stomach. It's also fun to string the cereal on a piece of thin yarn about twelve inches long. Leave enough yarn to tie a knot. Hang this necklace on a tree outside the patient's window for the birds to eat.

10. Flavored gelatin is more fun when it's prepared in a nine-by-twelve-inch cake pan. Use cookie cutters to cut fun figures for the patient to eat. Dry toast also tastes better when it's cut into shapes.

11. Brighten your child's room; decorate it with colored crepe paper, and tape a cheery poster to the ceiling.

12. Prepare alphabet soup and encourage a young child to find the letters of his or her name or spell words on a spoon.

13. Encourage family members to create get-well cards to slip under the patient's door or put on a meal tray.

14. See if the child's class will make get-well cards, if he or she is going to be out for surgery or has had an accident that will keep the child confined for a while.

15. Write messages of encouragement on note paper and slip them on the night stand or pillow while the sick child is sleeping.

16. If the child's recuperation period is going to be several days, give him or her new things to do or special food treats gift-wrapped as surprises.

17. Request your children's school work. They can work on it at their own pace and won't feel so overloaded when they return to school.

Fun Activities for Sick Days
18. Create a Sunshine Sick Box. A shoe box works well, or you can use a nine-by-twelve-inch

metal cake pan with a plastic lid. Decorate the lid of the shoebox with cute gift-wrap paper. Or the child may enjoy decorating the plastic lid with colored acrylic markers. Fill the box with a new activity or coloring book, crayons, fun stickers, pad of paper, watercolors or cassette tape with good stories or music.

19. Buy a kaleidoscope or View Master to occupy a small child confined to bed.

20. Younger children will enjoy a play doctor's kit to nurse their stuffed animals.

21. Older children might enjoy a model or craft project to work on while they're recovering.

22. Read a new book or an old favorite aloud to your child.

23. Play board games or work puzzles with the patient.

24. Get out family albums and pictures to look at together. Tell your child stories about what he or she did when younger.

25. Reminisce about a favorite vacation, the attractions and highlights of the trip. Then write scrambled words about the trip on paper. For example, if your family visited New York, your words might be: het utteas fo yblrtie; snrtga botm; drawyboa. (The answers are The Statue of Liberty, Grant's Tomb and Broadway.)

Chapter 15

Character Builders

Children are growing up in a fast-paced, transitional society with rapidly changing expectations and values. They're barraged with viewpoints that force them to question their values and yours. It's important to give them a sound standard with which to make decisions and to measure an idea's merit.

When the Peels' ten-year-old son came home after spending the night with a new friend, he appeared troubled. He told Bill and Kathy that the movie the family watched was not one they would allow at their home, but he didn't know what to do. He said, "I turned my head during the bad parts. I thought if I said something or left the room they might think I was rude."

Their son's experience gave the Peels an ideal opportunity to discuss, as a family, how to handle awkward situations like this in the future. The boys suggested that they ask their host or hostess if it would be all right to go into the other room and look for something else to do. If they were

"First I make my decisions; then my decisions make me."

Howard Hendricks

questioned, they would respectfully say that they didn't feel they would be allowed to watch that movie at home. Bill and Kathy affirmed their boys suggestions and added that if they were in a situation where they felt pressured to do something wrong, they should call home and the Peels would come get them.

If you teach your children the importance of making wise decisions, they'll have a head start in life. The most time-honored book of wisdom is the Bible. Children can learn from an early age that the Creator of the universe knows best how we operate, so it's always a good idea to follow the manufacturer's instructions.

Here are some ideas to encourage character growth in your children:

1. Practice the principles you want your children to embrace. If you want them to learn it, you need to live it. Children, however, won't care about the values we hold unless they know how much we care about them.

2. Listen to your children and pray with them about difficult circumstances and concerns just before they go to bed. Psychologists tell us this is one of the most impressionable times of the day. It's also a good time to express what we appreciate about our children. Often they struggle with feelings of failure, especially if they have difficulty at school. Acknowledge those feelings, and discuss ways to live with or solve the problems. Encourage your children by letting them know the special qualities and gifts you see in them.

3. Prepare a special dinner and time of dedication for a child or family member who is embarking on a new venture. This might include the new school year, school officer's position, new job, part in a play, speech tournament, class trip or participation on a sports team.

4. Encourage your child to keep a journal and prayer diary. It helps to express feelings and clarify thoughts on paper. Faith is built and strengthened when your child can go back over a diary and see how God has answered prayer.

5. Invite your children's youth workers or Sunday school teachers for dinner, so you and your child can have an opportunity to get to know them better. Let the kids send out invitations and help prepare and serve the meal.

6. Watch the *McGee and Me!* videos for children. These thirty-minute movies are action-packed, humorous adventures. And they teach valuable principles in a way children can relate to and understand. A helpful discussion booklet for parents about the characters, story and lessons learned is also included. Our kids invite neighborhood children over to watch these worthwhile adventures. (The *McGee and Me!* series is available at Christian bookstores.)

7. Create a Swine Fine jar to reinforce proper behavior and etiquette. Anyone caught using bad manners or offensive language deposits a quarter in a quart jar. Keep a sheet of paper by the jar for the offender to record his or her name. The person with the least number of Swine Fines at the end of the month keeps the quarters. Mom and Dad play, too. If you have a particular behavior problem you want to correct, work specifically on that for the month. For example, in the all-sons Peel house, the offender gives Mom a quarter for ungentlemanly behavior.

8. Help your children think through what they would do in certain situations that test their values or their ability to make decisions regarding their own safety.

One time Joy's son, John Mark, was accidentally locked in a foot locker by another friend. After Joy pried the lock open, she talked to the boys about the danger of climbing into containers that can close and lock. As a result of this incident and another emergency situation where a preschool son was caught alone in an elevator, Joy established "What would you do if. . .?" sessions with her kids.

This is a good way to help kids learn how to protect and take care of themselves in potentially hard or threatening situations. Try not to over-react when your children say things that shock and surprise you. Discuss an emergency game plan with them. If your children reveal to you that a certain situation is serious or that they have been violated in some way, seek the help of a counselor or pastor. Most of all, listen to your children's answers—what they're saying and not saying—and guide them gently into wise choices.

To stimulate communication with younger children, ask these questions. What would you do if:

—someone you don't know offers you something to eat or drink?

—a friend is locked in a closet or out of his or her house?

—you're lost in a store?

—someone touches you where you don't want to be touched?

—you're playing in the front yard when a stranger drives up and wants you to come over to the car window?

9. Use the following questions as a springboard for communication with older children. What would you do if:

—you were in a store with a friend, and you see him or her take something and not pay for it?

—you go to a party and alcoholic beverages and drugs are being offered?

—your friend tells you he cheated on the test he just finished?

—your crowd of friends asks you to do something you know isn't right?

—you're asked to watch a TV program or movie at a friend's house that would not be allowed at home?

—a friend tells you he or she is having sex with someone?

—an adult you don't know, a friend of the fam-

ily or someone near your own age acts too familiar and makes sexual suggestions to you?

—someone asks you to go with him or her but warns you not to tell your parents?

—someone threatens to harm you or writes you a threatening note?

—your friend is talking about committing suicide?

10. Institute Start the Day Off Right Family Table Talks. The Peels make this part of their regular breakfast routine. First, read a quote aloud and ask the kids to tell you what they think it means. Second, read a brief Scripture passage. Then ask, "What principles might God be trying to teach us through the verses? How can we apply these principles or truths to our activities today?" Third, pray, asking God to teach the family these truths and to incorporate them into their lives.

The following table talks, which include a quotation, verses and a prayer, show how simple the format is:

Day One

"The bigger a man's head gets, the easier it is to fill his shoes."[1]

Henry A. Courtney

"When pride comes, then comes disgrace, but with humility comes wisdom"[2]

Lord, you have given us the abilities we have. Help us remember that without you we are nothing.

Day Two

"Better to remain silent and to be thought a fool than to speak out and remove all doubt."[3]

Abraham Lincoln

"Even a fool is thought wise if he keeps silent, and discerning is he who holds his tongue."[4] "When words are many, sin is not absent, but he who holds his tongue is wise."[5]

Father, help us remember the power of our words and to speak only that which is helpful, kind and uplifting.

Day Three

"For of all sad words of tongue or pen, The saddest are these: 'It might have been!' "[6]
John Greenleaf Whittier

"Be very careful, then, how you live—not as unwise but as wise, making the most of every opportunity, because the days are evil"[7]

Lord, we thank you for the privilege of being alive today. Help us to use our time wisely and to make the most of this day.

Day Four

"One can never consent to creep when one feels an impulse to soar."[8]
Helen Keller

"Keep away from people who try to belittle your ambitions. Small people always do that, but the really great make you feel that you, too, can become great."[9]
Mark Twain

"I can do everything through him who gives me strength."[10]

Heavenly Father, today we ask that you help us do those things that are difficult for us to do. You are a big God, and we need your help. Don't let us be content to creep along in any area of our lives; enable us to soar to new heights, so that we may become all that you want us to be.

Day Five

"When we are not acceptable to ourselves, we have a greater desire to be acceptable to others."
George MacDonald

"For you created my inmost being; you knit me together in my mother's womb. I praise you because I am fearfully and wonderfully made; your works are wonderful, I know that full well."[11]

Thank you, Lord, for the way you made me. Help me to use my special gifts in a positive and productive way. Use me today to help others feel good about who they are, and let me encourage them to reach their full potential.

1. Henry A. Courtney, *Bits & Pieces* (May 1989), vol. 22, no. 5, 8.
2. Proverbs 11:2.
3. Auriel Douglas, Michael Strumpf, *Webster's New World Best Book of Aphorisms* (New York: Arco Publishing, Inc., 1989), 90.
4. Proverbs 17:28.
5. Proverbs 10:19.
6. Douglas, *Webster's New World*, 113.
7. Ephesians 5:15,16.
8. Douglas, *Webster's New World*, 27.
9. Ibid.
10. Philippians 4:13.
11. Psalm 139:13,14.

Chapter 16

Filling Your Own Tank

For women who choose household administration as a career, measuring fabric softener and looking at a bottoms-up child half the day doesn't really tax the gray matter. They salivate at the thought of an adult conversation after spending sixteen hours a day with a whining three-year-old. Even though they love and are deeply committed to their children, sometimes they fear their brain may atrophy. Having time to learn something new or to read a good book seem like fantasies.

Those women with careers have little advantage. After a day at the office, they return home to a host of responsibilities that drain whatever resolve they have left. Most nights they're so tired that watching TV is an easy escape.

Here are some suggestions to help you fill up your own tank instead of watching your energy gauge steadily decline to empty:

1. Set a goal to learn something new every day. If you have four children under five tugging at

"The two things children wear out are clothes and parents."

Anonymous

your skirt all day, you may only be able to devote ten to fifteen minutes a day to learning.

2. Keep a notebook with tabbed divisions, so you can organize your activities. It saves time, allows you to accomplish more and helps you feel less chaotic and more in control. Take this notebook with you everywhere, so you can immediately check on and write down appointments. Here are some sections you might include: a monthly calendar to record events, a to-do list, birthdays and gifts, children, clothing sizes for family members, home maintenance, ideas for projects, personal goals, phone numbers and addresses and travel information.

3. Decide on realistic personal goals for yourself this year, regarding how you want to grow intellectually, spiritually, physically, socially and emotionally. Set aside a specific time daily or weekly to work on those goals. Set a date in the

future to reassess them. Sometimes you may discover that whatever you have set out to do doesn't work or you don't enjoy doing it. You may also find that a goal can't be accomplished because of other demands or critical changes in your circumstances. This doesn't mean you have failed; it just means you need to re-evaluate your goals and set new ones you can meet.

4. If you have young children at home, trade off taking care of kids with other moms and dads. Spend some of this time learning a new skill.

5. One mother of three preschoolers places open devotional books and Bibles in each room of her house. As she carries out her never-ending duties, she snatches a bit of inspiration to keep her going.

6. Use your time wisely in the afternoon when your preschoolers nap or have a quiet time in their rooms. Turn off the TV, turn on the phone answering machine, fix a cup of tea, prop up your feet and pick up a good book or catch up on current events. Children who don't nap need to understand that parents need time to rest and regroup. Train children to play quietly in their rooms for forty-five minutes. Set a kitchen timer. When it rings, their quiet time is over. This will help prevent the constant begging about when they can come out to play.

7. Spend time with other parents who have older children and values compatible with yours. The experience of these parents will help you define what is normal and what could be a potential problem in rearing your children.

8. Decide now what kind of a grandparent you want to be. We met a young seventy-six-year-old woman who was devoting her time to taking her grandchildren on educational trips. She began para-sailing when she was seventy-two.

9. The average American spends twenty-seven hours a year sitting at red lights.[1] Recognize this opportunity and listen to audio books or educational tapes when you're in the car. In only six years, you will have the equivalent of three years of college.

10. Make the most of your time. Take something good to read or a portable project you can work on everywhere you go. Grab moments to work on it while you're waiting for the carpool or in the doctor's office.

11. Allow yourself the freedom to dream. Is there something you have always wanted to do? One woman went back to college when her youngest turned eighteen. In her late forties, she graduated and started a new career. Your kids may be small now, but taking one college class or specialized course toward your desired dream will prepare you for unexpected opportunities in the future.

12. Take an extension course at a local college or enroll in a correspondence course in a subject you have always wanted to study just for fun. Some colleges also televise classes, so you can take them right in your home.

13. Network with other parents who share your interest in the arts, crafts, gourmet cooking,

history, literature, mechanical projects, music or writing. Take classes or do projects together. Hold each other accountable to spend a certain time each week doing your favorite activity.

14. Develop your own emotional health. The guilt, hurt or shame of a parent is often expressed in anger or bitterness toward a child. Every child deserves wholeness. If you need help, find a support group or counseling center to help you work through your pain.

1. Lewis Timberlake, *Born to Win* (Wheaton: Tyndale House Publishers, 1986), 125.

Dear Moms and Dads,

We hope that the ideas in this manual have helped you make the school year a more rewarding experience and create an atmosphere in your home that enables your children to reach their full potential.

We would also love to hear about your adventures in child rearing. Send us your humorous stories, creative ideas and suggestions on how to make family life run smoother.

Write to us at:
Creative Alternatives
P.O. Box 5100
Tyler, Texas 75712

The authors and their families. (From left, bottom) The Mahaffeys: Joy, John Mark, Kristi, Mac, (back row) Bill and Mark; The Peels: (from left, top front) James, (back row) John, Joel, Kathy and Bill.

Kathy Peel, president of Creative Alternatives, speaks on parenthood, creativity and how to be an entrepreneur. Kathy, who has been married for 19 years, graduated from Southern Methodist University and is presently pursuing a master's degree in journalism-speech communications.

Joy Mahaffey, also married for 19 years, holds a master's degree from North Texas State University in speech pathology. She speaks to women's groups and retreats, substitute teaches and practices speech pathology part-time.